RESILIENC

Leadership wit

Éditions Favre SA
Head office:
29, rue de Bourg
CH-1002 Lausanne
Tel: (+41) 021 312 17 17
lausanne@editionsfavre.com
www.editionsfavre.com

Groupe Libella, Paris

Legal deposit in Switzerland for the original edition in French under the title *Quotient résilience*, November 2021.

Translation: Frank Gerritzen
Illustrations: Sophie Conchon
Layout and graphic design: Dynamic 19

ISBN: 978-2-8289-1975-7

Éditions Favre receives structural support from the Federal Office of Culture for the years 2021-2024.

Alexia Michiels

RESILIENCE QUOTIENT

Leadership with heart and purpose

Translated into English by Frank Gerritzen

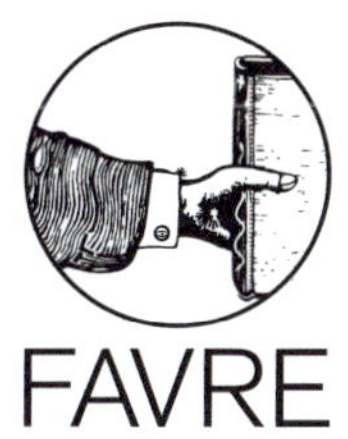

FAVRE

To our children

OVERVIEW

PREAMBLE

In 2017, I published my first book *The Resilience Drive*, guided by the enthusiasm for sharing simple strategies, resilience habits, whose effectiveness is proven by research. It seemed useful to me to take a scientific look at common sense practices that are often overseen in the hustle and bustle of everyday life. I also wanted to offer a preventive perspective of resilience, based on the opportunity to fully mobilize all of our resources – body, heart, mind, and spirit.

The 100 simple practices suggested in this first book are essentially levers of personal resilience.

Today, my remarks are complementary, and my motivation is different. Of course, the recent global situation and the Covid-19 pandemic have brought the concept of resilience to the forefront, at the personal, organizational, and societal levels. The activities of the Resilience Institute, which I co-founded in Europe, have benefited from this - quite sudden - awareness within organizations. The topic of resilience was no longer trivial but a priority. It was vital to raise awareness among employees, develop coping strategies for managers and ensure business continuity.

It has become increasingly obvious to me that the leader's role – team leader, director, or manager (more on these terms later) – is crucial and critical to the collective resilience capacity of a team. However, the required skills to lead a team courageously, benevolently, and successfully in today's world are not all present. School, continuous education, university and corporate training programs rarely incorporate these skills of a different kind, which I call *resilience skills*.

The desire grew to write about it and to humbly offer a distinct perspective on leadership skills. This book is the outcome of twenty years of professional experience, including twelve years at the Resilience Institute where I coach teams and leaders in their managerial role. I have witnessed with joy and confidence an ever-growing attention to resilience skills. In this publication, I want to emphasize the interpersonal dimension, and so reminding us how influential a leader's behavior is on his staff.

This book is for anyone who oversees a team – whether small, medium, or large. For simplicity's sake, and to remain gender neutral, I often use the term *manager* or *leader* which identifies both men and women. For the ease of reading, I have decided not to use inclusive language but to use the masculine form.

It goes without saying that when *leader* or *manager* are mentioned, it applies to all genders.

Hopefully, you will find some food for thought and, above all, some courses of action to strengthen your impact and positively influence your staff.

Whether you run a construction site, a hair salon, a law firm, a fashion boutique, a restaurant, a school, a multinational corporation, or train people, if you have employees or interns in your care, this book is for you.

FOREWORD
by Ilham Kadri
CEO and President of Solvay's Executive Committee

We are living a true leadership transformation. The world around us is rapidly changing: "global," "uncertain," "volatile," "fast," "agile," "well-being," "burn-out" or "bore-out" are words that are part of our daily lives as business leaders. As a result, we see new business cultures, new codes, purposes, new ways of working, and new focuses, notably on well-being, coming from leaders that navigate change and manage their teams differently than before. Resilience, which is brilliantly decoded in this book, is the key for any leader to face new challenges, stay grounded, remain his/her true self and outperform in the long-run. Ultimately, resilient leaders evolve with their time but they have a strong sense of self, their relationship to others, their environment, and the question of meaning, as Alexia Michiels describes it.

Simply put, the leadership styles of yesterday are not adequate to meet the challenges we face today. Today's leaders must be resilient. They must have empathy. They must lead with their hearts as well as their minds.

I strongly believe in the mindset of bringing one's whole self to work, which I find intrinsically linked to Alexia Michiels' perception of an authentic leader. Of course, the book highlights other types of leadership, but I feel best aligned with Alexia's definition of an authentic leadership, where truthfulness, authenticity, sincerity and humility prevail. In my view, to lead with your heart and your mind you need to bring your whole self to work every day. This is not an easy task. Bringing your whole self to work every day takes a lot of courage. It means breaking down emotional barriers and daring to be vulnerable, empathetic, imperfect, and authentic. Vulnerability is a strength not a weakness!

This mindset is not in opposition with professionalism, performance or success. Quite the contrary, if you are yourself at work you will perform at your best. At Solvay we have made the principle of bringing your whole self to work the foundation of our diversity, equity and inclusion roadmap. For instance, when I switch on my computer in the mornings, I am more than a businesswoman in a suit: I am still a mother. I was born and raised in Morocco. I have strong convictions. These things are all part of who I am at work and they play a strong role in my ability to lead.

I want today's leaders at Solvay to nurture a mindset in which they and everyone around them feels empowered to be themselves, speak up, and unleash their full potential. Making people feel valued and respected for who they are creates a more satisfying, sustainable environment. We're bringing human dignity back to the center of everything we do. I believe that companies that put human dignity first will last the longest.

Alexia's book also highlights the importance of finding your purpose to strengthen your own resilience and the resilience of your company. This is a message very close to my heart. Since the beginning of my mandate as a CEO, in 2019, as a bottom up exercise we sought out our "*why*". When you ask someone *"why"* they are doing their job, they often end up telling you the *"what"* and the *"how"*, rather than the *"why"*. After a nine-month listening exercise, we unveiled our new vision – sustainable shared value for all – and our purpose – we bond people, elements and ideas to reinvent progress. Beyond our financial imperatives, our purpose encapsulates why we exist, what is our North Star as a company. Our Vision is what the world will look like when we fully live our purpose.

Finally, the importance of making bold business decisions while still caring for people is another element of Alexia Michiels' book that especially stands out. It's about the power of AND. As business leaders we must believe in the intriguing concept that we have the courage, curiosity and long term perspective to operate within two seemingly opposed ideas: we can be inspired by our past AND engaged in our future; we can be humble AND bold; profitable AND sustainable; science-driven AND innately human; caring AND daring.

This kind of resilient leadership is especially crucial to meet the most pressing challenges we face, such as the climate emergency, environmental deterioration, resource scarcity, social inequalities, growing population, political upheavals, as Alexia points out. Through strong, people centered leadership we can unleash the full potential of our teams and drive innovations that will bring down our greenhouse gas emissions, create the circular economy solutions of the future, enable a better life for all and be profitable.

As leaders today we have a huge responsibility to inspire the next generation of leaders and live up to their expectations. It is up to us to create better leaders and, as a result, a better world. This book provides an excellent blueprint that will inspire any leader to understand how one can activate purpose at the service of causes that are bigger than us.

INTRODUCTION

Since it is at the heart of this book and punctuates most of the chapters, the notion of *resilience* deserves to be explored and clarified. The English word *resilience* comes from the Latin *resilire*, to rebound, to reflect on.

The Merriam-Webster dictionary provides several definitions to help us think about the term. In physics, resilience is the ability of a material to recover its initial shape after a shock. The famous psychiatrist and author Boris Cyrulnik reminds us of the first use of the word in the field of geology: farmers describe soil as resilient when, after a flood or a fire, life resumes but not quite as before. It is an adaptive transformation; a *catastrophe* forcing a change of direction. What a great metaphor! In psychology, resilience is the ability of an individual to psychically resist the trials of life, to bounce back, to rebuild. In computer science, it is the capacity of a system to continue to function, despite a breakdown. In ecology, resilience defines the capacity of an ecosystem, a biotope, or a group of individuals to recover after an external disturbance. At the Resilience Institute, we define resilience as a set of skills allowing us to bounce back, grow through challenges, make a positive impact beyond ourselves, and achieve fulfillment. Quite a program! Vast, yes, but exhilarating!

Resilience invites you to fully mobilize all of your resources – body, heart, mind, and spirit – to navigate through the ups and downs of life with more confidence, joy, and success.

The resilience spiral is an invitation to become aware of your state, or the state of your team, in order to choose the best response to a situation. Negative spirals are part of life; it is illusory to try to avoid them at all costs. However, being alert

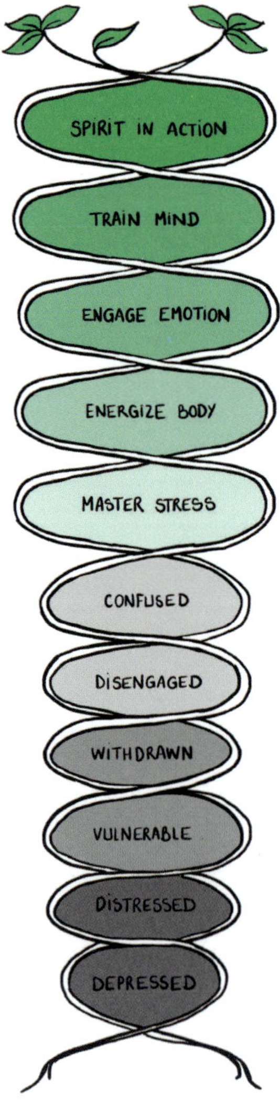

and capable of not remaining stuck in a negative state is within your reach. Similarly, being always at the top and seeking permanent happiness at all costs is either naive or arrogant.

Being resilient means knowing yourself, recognizing that every state (and indeed, life itself!) is temporary (impermanent) and creating the conditions allowing you to spend more time in the positive – more fulfilling – spiral.

This is true for a team as well as for an entire organization. My hypothesis is that a team leader, through his behavior and attitude, greatly influences the behavior and attitude the team exhibits. This is what I have observed in a number of situations. Leaders: this is why this book is for you, whose impact on a team is often greater than you can imagine.

The recent evolution of the world has revealed the notion of interdependence in a clearer way, and it can no longer be denied. Interdependence between human beings and nature, between countries, between economic, political, scientific, and social sectors. Guiding a team with benevolence, with resilience, implies taking this interdependence into account. It encompasses considering all the stakeholders of a project in order to better lead it. This is a far more complex task than acting in ignorance, but a much more satisfying one!

After a first chapter dealing with the current situation, the next chapters of this book are designed as reflection stages: relation to oneself, relation to others, relation to the environment and finally, the question of meaning. This journey seems relevant and necessary. Each stage counts to better embrace the next.

Throughout the chapters, *reflection breaks* will punctuate your reading. Given the often-hectic pace of our busy days, these moments tend to be few or nonexistent. We are naturally more reactive than responsive. This attitude is not up to the challenges of today's world. Creating time to reflect is a real discipline that needs nurturing in order to make better decisions.

Finally, you will find a *Practical Menu* to translate these ideas into action. You will discover some suggestions aimed at strengthening your *Resilience Quotient* and cultivating a thoroughly human leadership.

CHAPTER 1

NAVIGATING UNCERTAINTY

"To understand is not to understand everything, it is also acknowledging that there is something incomprehensible."

Edgar Morin

Today´s world – less clarity, more awareness

The recent evolution of the world has upset the convictions of those who believed that Science and Man are stronger than nature. This is a call to humility – a virtue that has grown rarer during the last hundred years. This stretch of time is marked, among other things, by the multiplication of scientific progress, material well-being, acceleration of production rates, expansion of cities and the desertification of the countryside. We must face a growing disconnection between human activity and the cycles of nature, without denying the progress of modern civilization – for example in healthcare.

Managerial responsibility and the related skill sets must evolve. The Covid-19 pandemic has highlighted our extraordinary resilience ability! In the midst of the ordeal, a great many people and organizations have mobilized undervalued resources and demonstrated notable resilience in record time.

In the professional world, remote work has become widespread at an unprecedented speed. Many organizations have successfully implemented systems that ensure business continuity despite the constraints of (partial) lockdown. Leaders have shown extraordinary responsiveness in guiding their teams remotely, maintaining contact "while away" and pursuing their goals. This "performance" has an undeniable human cost: the blurred boundaries between home and work tend to generate more work and, for some, great difficulty in disconnecting. Mental health is on the line, and no one is invincible. As a leader, you cannot ignore this situation; while many non-work factors are at play in these matters, it is your responsibility to create a – possibly virtual – work environment that sustains the resilience and mental health of your employees.

The unknown and the doubts bring out salutary realizations.

The global situation remains *volatile, uncertain, complex, and ambiguous* (summarized by the acronym "VUCA").

Confrontation with the unknown and unpredictable tends to revive a form of humility. I dare state that the Covid-19 pandemic has underscored the inconsistencies of an unsustainable system and the need to accelerate the transformation of our lifestyles and our ways of working.

The various theories of resilience identify *type 1* resilience, consisting in mobilizing the necessary energies to find the *status quo ante* balance and *type 2* resilience, which consists in initiating a process of transformation prompting the person, organization or society to grow through hardship. It is obviously the latter perspective that I encourage you to consider. Even if resilience can be natural (some people are genetically more resilient than others), there is no doubt that a large number of resilience skills are acquired; it depends on the environment, learning and education.

With no further ado, it is now necessary to nurture our resilience skills, to bring reflexive answers in order to question our way of living, working and managing a team. Beyond the purely rational, we need to solicit skills that have been underused, dormant or simply undervalued in the professional world. In a global setting that is due to remain very uncertain, I believe these skills will be markers of success.

All the while keeping past good practices, priorities need to be repositioned. The time is right to insist on the importance of relationships and to pursue the quest for meaning, sharpened by turbulent times.

Let us take advantage of crises to change the system, ask ourselves the right questions, and make more conscious choices about the impacts of our behaviors and decisions, beyond ourselves. Individually, through our actions, we can help build the world of tomorrow.

And the manager in all this?

If you are reading this book, you are probably responsible for a team. Whether it is a small team or an entire organization, you are a manager, a leader.

Chief, manager, leader... what are we actually talking about?

Everyone probably has an intuitive understanding of what leadership means. One's perception of the term has evolved dramatically over the past 100 years, at the discretion of fashions, ideologies and the transformation of society and professional environments.

The word *leader* is of English origin and refers to a *chief*. The Merriam-Webster dictionary defines a leader as a person who has commanding authority or influence.

Early definitions of leadership emphasize control, centralization of power, authority, and a guiding line based on dominance relationships, a very vertical and hierarchical perspective of the word.

The leader is the "one who knows" – the expert – guiding the group.

Gradually, the idea of a *leader's influence* emerges; leadership is then defined as the behavior of an individual, the leader, who influences other individuals or a group in the pursuit of common goals.

Over the last twenty years, novel trends have proposed different approaches to the definition, emphasizing different attributes of the leader.

For example:

Authentic leadership, valuing the authenticity and sincerity of the leader as well as those of his team.

Servant leadership, which positions a leader at the service of his employees, helping them develop autonomy and competency.

Spiritual leadership, emphasizing personal and group values.

These different trends underline the importance of emotional skills, long considered marginal in a professional environment. Many organizations recognize that emotional intelligence is one of the key competencies of high performers. Daniel Goleman, a world expert on emotional intelligence, advocates that

85% of the skills accounting for the highest performance in leaders are due to emotional intelligence – the balance being technical skills[1].

1 D. GOLEMAN, *Working with emotional intelligence*, Bantam, 2000.

Leading a team, with your head, your heart and more

For over a hundred years, understanding, defining, and measuring human intelligence has been the subject of various research studies. In the early 20th century, the Frenchman Alfred Binet (1857-1911) developed the first intelligence evaluation to characterize children with learning difficulties. His test assumed that intelligence evolves with age but remains relatively stable compared to a group of peers of the same age.

IQ first - Intelligence Quotient

The concept of IQ has progressed over the years. A German psychologist, William Stern (1871-1938), formulated the first definition of IQ in 1912. He advanced the idea of expressing the results of intelligence tests with a number, the *intelligence quotient*. This number relates an estimated *mental age* to a current *present age*. For example, if a 10-year-old girl has the intellectual capacity of a 12-year-old girl, her IQ is 120 (12/10):

100 x mental age / chronological age

This equation only makes sense for children. It is estimated that about 50% of the world population has an average IQ (i.e., 90 to 110), about 13% is between 110 and 139 and 1.5% of the earth´s inhabitants have the IQ of a genius.

Stanford University professor Lewis Madison Terman (1877-1956) and David Wechsler (1896-1981) later carried forward the Binet test to measure adult intelligence. These assessments measure a range of cognitive abilities – vocabulary, mathematical skills, short-term memory, long-term memory, spatial perception, and reasoning skills.

The many IQ tests detractors believe that intelligence becomes whatever one decides to measure. The American psychologist Edwin Boring (1886-1968) stated: "Intelligence is what the tests test".

One of the fundamental questions is to distinguish between the part of intelligence linked to genes, the innate, and the part linked to experience and teaching, the acquired. Or said differently, *nature* versus *nurture*. It is highly likely that a favorable environment at key development stages has a profound impact on our intelligence. Some studies even demonstrate the influence of diet on the improvement of cognitive performance! Although many questions remain about the development of human intelligence, research has progressed and shifted the concept beyond cognitive skills.

Then the EQ - Emotional Quotient

The term "emotional intelligence" appeared in the 1960s, mentioned in publications specialized in psychology. In 1983, the American psychologist Howard Gardner (1943-) caused a stir by publishing the book *Frames of Mind: the Theory of Multiple Intelligences*. He suggests that IQ does not fully explain a child's cognitive abilities and introduces the concept of "multiple intelligences" – seven types of intelligence, complemented in 1993 with an eighth type, naturalistic.

The first mention of the term *emotional quotient* – EQ – to a wide audience appeared in an article published by Keith Beasley in 1987, in a British magazine[2]. He defined EQ as the ability to *feel* and IQ as the ability to *think*. In other words, **EQ is to the heart what IQ is to the brain**.

Finally in the 90's, the term *emotional intelligence* became widespread with the 1995 publication of Daniel Goleman's (1946-) book *Emotional Intelligence*. Like Howard Gardner, he asserts that a person's IQ, in setting aside an essential part of a human being's behavior - the emotions - is not sufficient to define his intelligence, and even less to predict his success. For Daniel Goleman, emotional intelligence encompasses self-awareness, self-management, social awareness, and relationship management. Goleman submits that it is a better predictor of success and achievement than IQ.

To this day, IQ tests are still widely used as a measurement of intelligence. However, the importance of EI is now recognized, including in professional environments. Recognizing and understanding emotions, regulating one's own, and managing those of others are essential skills for leading a team.

In 2018, researchers from UNIGE (University of Geneva - Switzerland) and UNIBE (University of Bern - Switzerland) developed an evaluation of emotional intelligence in a professional situation - *the Geneva Emotional Competence Test*[3]. This test attempts to assess and predict an employee's aptitude and leadership skills in interpersonal relationships. This ever-evolving evaluation hopes to scientifically validate its predictive aspect : a person's future in his or her professional career.

---

2 K. BEASLEY, "The emotional quotient", *Mensa Magazine* p. 25 (1987).

3 University of Geneva, Swiss Center for Affective Sciences, https://www.unige.ch/cisa/emotional- competence/home/research-tools/geco/

The inclusion of emotional engagement in the definition of intelligence opens the way to the integration of all human resources to define the competencies of the leader.

Last but not least, the RQ - Resilience Quotient

Continuous research in neuroscience, psychology and biology has refined our understanding of the human being. Simultaneously, a complex and changing professional background requires a skill set that was less necessary fifty years ago.

Given the current level of uncertainty, and considering the multiple challenges of this world, no leader can claim to have universal answers. This is a call to humility – the humility to know one's limits, accept doubt, and reveal one's vulnerability.

Leading a team today requires deeply human, intrapersonal, interpersonal and *beyond personal* skills. It is about bouncing back from adversity quickly, growing as a team through challenges, giving everyone an opportunity for fulfillment and have a positive impact beyond oneself.

What we define as resilience skills – under the name RQ *Resilience Quotient* – begins with being aware of one's own ecosystem.

The leader's ecosystem – within and beyond himself

Etymology often sheds more light than any elaborate definition. The word *ecosystem* comes from two Greek words: *oikos* meaning "house", and *systêma* meaning "assembly, composition, organization". *Ecosystem* therefore means "organization of the house". We are at the heart of our subject!

We strive to understand a system formed by an environment (biotope) and by all the species (biocenosis) that inhabit it. Applied to oneself, this term implies the understanding and management of our own "system" with all its constituent resources: body, heart, mind and spirit.

Within a family or an organization, we are all part of a *system* whose parts are linked by a tight mesh, allowing them to act effectively.

By gaining some height – literally and figuratively – it becomes obvious that the universe is an ecosystem in which societies, organizations, human beings are linked together by their affiliation to this common *house* and are therefore interdependent.

How does this influence the management of a team? It is quite straightforward, because understanding the ecosystem concept and the interdependence of its components fundamentally changes (or should change) the way leaders take decisions.

My awareness of the interactions between the resources that constitute my own person enables more conscious choices and improved self-management.

Considering the *systemic aspect* of an organization leads to my taking particular care of the quality of the relationships I establish within my team.

Finally, understanding human beings and organizations as components of a *universal system* invites us to bear responsibility for the influence of our decisions on ourselves, on others, and on the environment. To ignore this interdependence is to ignore what binds us together, and all of us to the environment.

Inspired by this ecosystem concept, I have chosen, in the coming chapters, to discuss the skills I believe are essential to manage a team with conscience and success.

Are you ready? Let us explore these deeply human skills called resilience skills, and so encourage you to lead your team... differently.

CHAPTER 2

RELATION WITH ONESELF

"Know thyself and you shall know the universe and the Gods"

Socrates

Knowing yourself well - the work of a lifetime

Socrates's philosophy is still radiating today. His invitation to introspection suggests that anyone possesses the gift of knowledge and understanding. This is Plato's theory of *reminiscence*, consisting of learning to remember. How does one achieve this? By self-questioning, by reflecting; what Socrates calls maieutic, a dialogue between the soul and oneself or between a student and a teacher. It is an effort of self-awareness.

It is both the starting point and the work of one's entire life. To know oneself deeply is a process bringing taste to life and substance to any human being. The second, often overlooked, part of the citation suggests that self-awareness is the path to better comprehend this world (and what is beyond).

Trying to lead a team while ignoring this personal approach is doomed to fail.

It may look like an evidence. Still, over the course of my professional career, I have met many leaders performing their managerial duties with conviction and sometimes (or frequently) little humility, who were totally disconnected from their own being. Empathy – a key-competence to which we shall revert in Chapter 3 – is based on self-awareness. To know oneself well to better understand others.

Self-awareness goes well beyond understanding one's own personality and the perception of one's strengths and weaknesses. It also includes the dimensions that constitute us : physical, emotional, mental, and spiritual. Although not a physician, I am fascinated by human biology – our physiology – which, in the end, explains *almost everything*. There is a fair share of mystery that I acknowledge and that leaves the door open to large fields of reflection.

On a day-to-day basis, thorough self-knowledge is an invitation to discern in which state of mind you are – right now. Research[4] suggests that self-awareness is a determining factor to reach self-control. This realization is rarely automatic; it is the result of a *freeze frame*.

This personal approach results in a more precise, more complete, and more holistic insight – a kind of reading grid that is consequently also applicable outside, in a professional environment and beyond. This systemic approach is more complex and requires a number of competences, which are discussed in this chapter.

4 R.E. BOYATZIS, M. BURCKLE, "Psychometric properties of the ECI"; Hay/McBer Group Boston (1999)

Bring your attention to the present moment and ask yourself these few questions:

- How is my body today? Am I fit, well-rested, energetic, or tense, tired and experiencing physical distress symptoms (back pain, migraine, upset stomach or other)?
- What emotions am I perceiving? Do I feel calm, joyful, confident, or rather agitated, frustrated, or angry? Emotions are plenty – try to identify those that you feel as precisely as possible.
- What thoughts are filling or bothering my mental space? Are these thoughts helping me or being of disservice? Are they sustaining my attention to the present moment or keeping me away from it?
- What is my general intention today? What do I want to focus on? What kind of attitude do I wish for myself for the day?

The 7 pillars of personal resilience

The Resilience Institute´s approach to resilience is integral, research-based and practical. The integral perspective suggests mobilizing all of our personal resources: body, heart, mind and spirit. It is a holistic approach of the human being, far removed from the Cartesianism that has dominated our Western societies for several centuries.

The philosopher René Descartes (1596-1650) considered thought the main attribute of man. In the perspective of today´s scientific knowledge, reducing Man to the cognitive dimension amounts to deprive him of an immense potential.

Knowing, acknowledging and understanding the interactions between our energy, our emotions and our thoughts opens up a fascinating field of development and is a first step towards nurturing our personal resilience.

Translating this knowledge into simple practices was the subject of my first book *The Resilience Drive* (Favre, 2017). I therefore choose here to recall the pillars of resilience in a synthetic way. These are based on the premise that we can make conscious choices. This capacity is what distinguishes us from animals which, as is assumed, live instinctively and reactively.

We cannot choose what happens to us, but we have the freedom to choose how we respond to what happens to us.

What an amazing realization!

Self-awareness is truly the first pillar of resilience. As described above, it is a daily endeavour.

An awareness that prompts you to regularly acknowledge your condition, that of your collaborators, that of your team. Those who wear blinkers and refuse to recognize their own situation will have trouble understanding the difficulties their team may be experiencing.

When you feel challenged – in a negative spiral – it is important to put into place winning behaviors. Practices that allow you to bounce back faster, higher. **This is the second pillar of resilience, the one that allows you to bounce back from hardship and emerge stronger** (see type 2 resilience – described in Chapter 1).

Below are some winning behaviors I encourage you to consider:

The other pillars of personal resilience resemble a virtuous journey that creates the conditions for self-actualization.

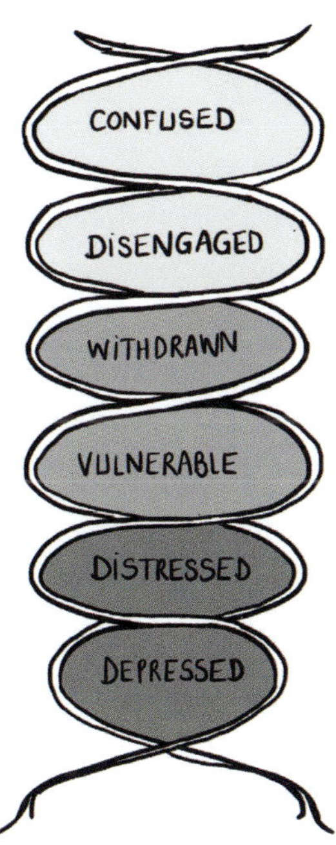

The third pillar is about creating calm and self-regeneration, diligently and intelligently. To keep pressure (commonly known as *stress*) positive, you must learn to master tactical calm and consider relaxation a true skill. The fourth pillar is about physical vitality and its various levers. I will focus more on these two pillars in the following pages.

Engaging your emotions is the fifth pillar of personal resilience. Emotions are physiological states that travel through us at all times of the day. Whether you like it or not, they influence you and your team. Emotions have a signature that also affects the cognitive dimension, the ability to collaborate, to be creative and to be focused, beyond the mood or atmosphere in a group. Positive psychology emphasizes the many benefits of positive emotions; we will come back to what this means for a leader in Chapter 3.

Training the mind is the sixth pillar of personal resilience. In my opinion, it is the most difficult to manage. Stimulated by an never-ending flow of information, our minds are in overdrive. This translates for some into a form of cerebral hyper-vigilance that interferes with sleep quality. The stimuli we ingest from morning to evening expose us to *infobesity* risk. On the positive side, neuroscience research has confirmed neuroplasticity, the brain's ability to constantly create new neuronal connections. This opens up extraordinary development pathways, including in your managerial role. We will touch on some of these in the next chapter.

The seventh pillar relates to the spiritual dimension - not in the religious sense, but in terms of ethics, values, and the meaning you give to your choices.

My personal experience coupled with observations I have made in organizations suggest that translating this spiritual dimension into a coherent behavior is not easy. It is simpler when I am rested, fit, rather positive and focused. In the context of a group - a company, a school or a hospital - how can we draw attention to meaning or values if the staff is exhausted? How can you expect calm and organized operations when most employees are agitated? How can you demand ethical behavior against a background of confusion or disengagement? Putting the spirit in action is ultimately the result of the care given to the previous six pillars. Which is why the relationship with the environment and the question of meaning is addressed in the last two chapters (chapters 4 and 5). Like Russian dolls that fit into each other, it seemed obvious to me that we must first nurture our relationship with ourselves to be able to nurture our relationship with others.

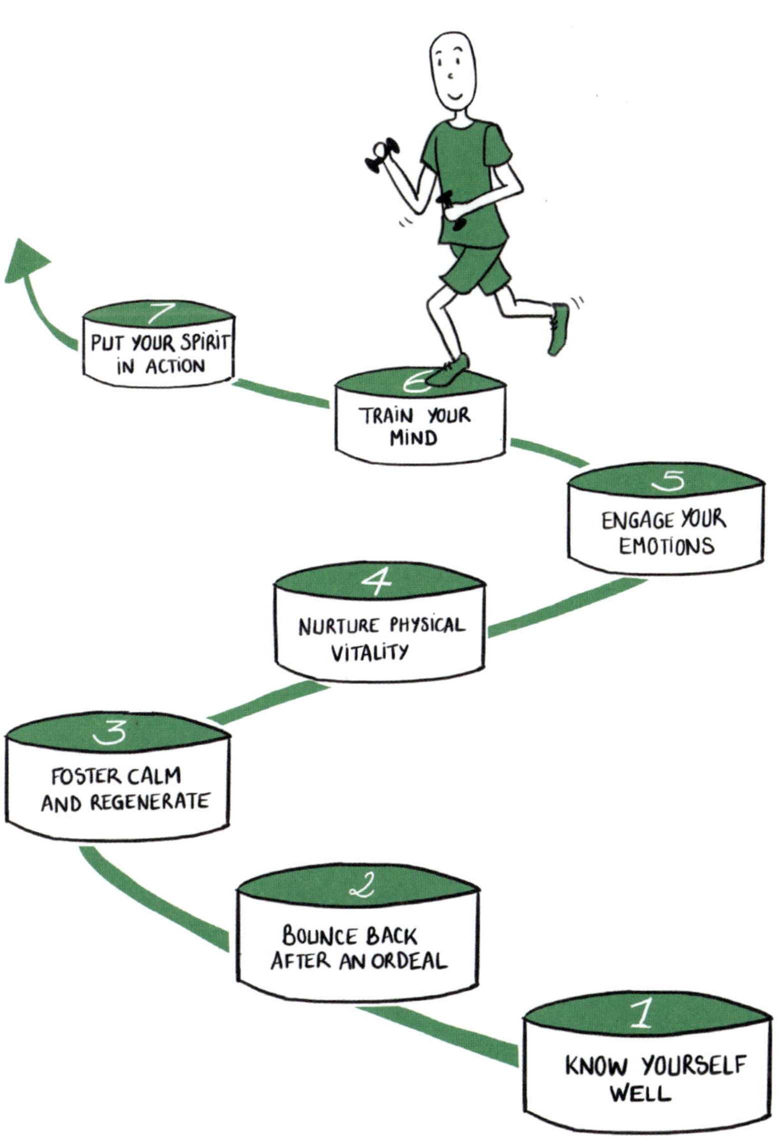
7
PUT YOUR SPIRIT IN ACTION
6
TRAIN YOUR MIND
5
ENGAGE YOUR EMOTIONS
4
NURTURE PHYSICAL VITALITY
3
FOSTER CALM AND REGENERATE
2
BOUNCE BACK AFTER AN ORDEAL
1
KNOW YOURSELF WELL

Our connection to the environment is based on the relationship with the other, by integrating the ecosystem in which we evolve. Questions about meaning can then come forward in the most constructive way. For this approach to be sustainable, we must first of all remain calm and in shape. In short, we must secure the base camp.

Securing the base camp - calm and vitality

In mountaineering terminology, the base camp is the place where an expedition prepares for a performance or a challenge. Merely making it to the base is not trivial and requires specific skills. For example, the Everest base camp (on the Nepalese side) is located at an altitude of 5364 meters. It takes 51 hours of hiking (about 14 days) to reach it.

The base camp of your resilience is your ability to deal with everyday life's stresses and strains calmly, and maintaining a good level of physical energy. The probability of regulating your emotions in a constructive way, keeping a clear mind, and acting according to your values, is much higher when you are calm and rested. When you are agitated and exhausted, how can you remain positive, focused and be guided by your values?

Isn't pressure good for "performance"? Absolutely!

The correlation between pressure and performance has long been established and is known as the *Yerkes-Dodson* law. American psychologists Robert M. Yerkes (1876-1956) and John Dillingham Dodson (1879-1955) developed a model in 1908, indicating that performance increases with mental and physiological pressure, but only up to a certain point.

Where there is no pressure, no deadlines, a form of boredom and loss of energy emerge. Yerkes and Dodson suggest that living without any pressure leads to entropy (loss of energy), even chaos. When there is very little pressure, performance is low; you are in a *relaxed* state. When pressure increases, your physiology makes the necessary adjustments to cope successfully; your mind is focused and your creativity is sharpened. You are in a state of *flow*, or positive stress. When pressure increases again, you adapt and your performance level is at its peak. This is a familiar scenario when you manage many projects, prepare several meetings, and deadlines are approaching. The perceived stress increases but you manage to mobilize the resources needed to deliver. This is a state you want to maintain.

When the pressure increases still, things become more difficult...Your mind thinks "yes, okay, I'll take on this extra project", but your physiological self is under great strain; the line between peak achievement and physiological distress will, rapidly or surreptitiously, trigger performance decline. Increased efforts will merely worsen the situation. You feel *distress* exhausting your body, mind and spirit. This is untenable. If you do not act quickly and rebound, your performance reaches the *failing* zone.

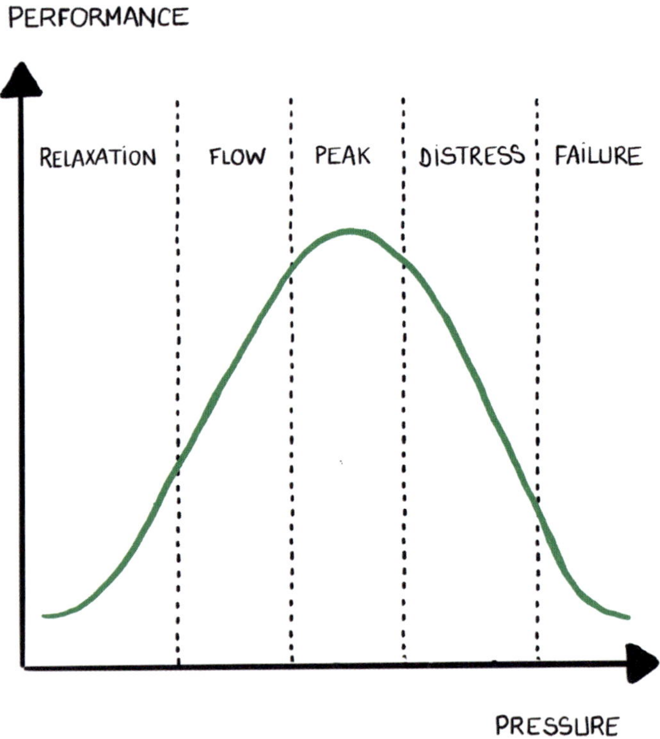

The analogy with elite athletes is useful. Their goal is to perform at top level during competition. In order to achieve this, and despite the immense pressure created by the stakes, they know that it is essential to include regeneration and recovery phases in their training plan. These athletes are coached to invite calm – even during a match! Watching tennis champions is instructive in this respect: when changing sides, the players sit on the bench for 2-3 minutes. This time is used to regenerate quickly and efficiently. Some – like Nadal – use rituals that, akin to Pavlov's reflex, put them in an almost instantaneous state of calm. The next time you watch Nadal on TV, you will notice that while sitting on the bench, he spends about 30 seconds pulling his socks up and down! Sometimes, he applies the same ritual between points as well.

Other athletes quietly practice a centering or breathing exercise to calm their physiology so as to be at the top of their game the next minute, ready to perform at their highest level. We call this tactical calm. The best athletes are able to move the curve up and to the right, not only through physical, but also mental training.

This is precisely what the practice of resilience also allows: successfully meeting challenges without the destructive effects of negative stress.

Relaxation is a true skill that you can develop. Creating calm and fostering quick regeneration are, in my opinion, instrumental skills for coping with the pressure of everyday life, and successfully facing the challenges that arise. In his book *Ascensions*[5] the former Nestlé CEO Peter Brabeck-Letmathe, tells how periods of doubt and insecurity can arise in a split second; in these extreme moments, it is crucial to keep calm, clear-headed and, above all, trust one's own abilities.

Your calmness is contagious; if you can spread serenity among your team, your employees are also more likely to remain calm, and thus achieve sustainable performance.

---

5 P. BRABECK-LETMATHE, *Ascensions*, Favre 2020.

Bring your attention to the present moment and ask yourself these few questions:

- In which zone do I spend most of my time during the work week - relaxation / flow / peak / distress or failure?
- What rituals or practices allow me to regenerate quickly and effectively?
- What is my favorite relaxation technique?
- What can I do in my team to create calmness?

Your base camp relies on your ability to stay calm, yes, but with energy!

Starting the day tired, even exhausted, is not only a painful experience for you, but also a predictor of inappropriate behaviors, of a mismatch between your aspirations and your actions.

A tired leader is not a good leader

Your energy level not only influences your general vitality but also your emotions, your thoughts, and therefore your behavior. In a state of exhaustion, you are not the best version of yourself. Your loved ones, your colleagues, your co-workers will pay the price.

Managing your energy level is a real skill

Among the different energy sources, such as energizing relationships, natural light, the joy of achieved goals, etc., I want to focus on three – that are within your reach and, more or less, within your control. Exercise and diet are evidently two essential sources of energy; the large body of research on these two sources highlights their impact, beyond vitality, on the emotional and cognitive dimensions. Scientific discoveries, in neuroscience especially, have revealed the multiple and multidimensional benefits of sleep, another fascinating subject! In short, notice that a good night's sleep impacts each of your organs and each of your biological functions positively; conversely, lack of sleep negatively influences your organs and your biological functions[6].

Move more, eat better! This well-known slogan is often used in public health promotion campaigns. It is nothing new... except that we have now identified the benefits of physical movement on mental health, and the influence of certain foods on our brain.

The Federation for Brain Research (FBR) has clearly demonstrated that regular exercise promotes a healthy brain function[7]. Physical movement improves mood, bolsters mental health, decreases the onset of cognitive problems and stimulates neural connections. Exercise increases levels of neurotransmitters such as serotonin, with its antidepressant effects, and has also a positive effect on sleep. Exercise stimulates the release of endorphins, which are responsible for the feeling of well-being felt after exercise, thus helping fighting depression, anxiety and feelings of negative stress.

Exercise is defined as "any movement of the body induced by the muscles that results in energy expenditure above that of rest". The WHO (World Health Organization) recommends 150 minutes of moderate-intensity exercise per week – or 30 minutes per day, 5 days a week[8].

---

6 M. WALKER, Why we sleep, *Scribner* (2018).

7 FRC (Brain Research Federation), https://www.frcneurodon.org/comprendre-le-cerveau/a-la- decouverte-du-cerveau/les-activites-physiques

8 WHO (World Health Organization), https://www.who.int/fr/news-room/fact-sheets/detail/physical- activity

Should your job require you to sit in front of a computer screen for long hours, simply getting up will boost your metabolism, as opposed to sitting without interruption for extended periods. Gretchen Reynolds, in her book *The First 20 Minutes*[9], suggests getting up every 20 minutes to prevent the physical aches and strains of sitting. This method can also improve your productivity as it gives a 20-minute deadline to complete certain tasks. The famous *pomodoro* technique (*tomato* in Italian – to symbolize a timer) promotes 5-minute breaks every 30 minutes. Simply getting up every 20 minutes is the easiest way to counteract the effects of a sedentary lifestyle; it boosts your metabolism and refreshes the mind. Stand-up or walking meetings are other tactics to fight inactivity.

The human being is not made to remain motionless; since the beginning of time, our body is destined to move!

What to eat to boost your energy and sustain your mental health?

Your body simply converts and uses the energy contained in your dietary nutrients. The quantity and quality of your food will obviously have a considerable impact on the proper functioning of all body functions – including the brain.

For optimal cognitive functioning, glucose supply to the neurons must be regular; therefore, ingredients with a low glycemic index are favored (legumes, whole-wheat bread and pasta, quinoa, green vegetables, etc.) and ingredients with a high glycemic index are limited (white bread, sweets, in particular).

Proteins (found in animal products, but also in legumes, nuts and seeds) are essential for communication between neurons, hence the performance of our cognitive abilities.

---

9 G. REYNOLDS, *The First 20 Minutes*, Avery (2013).

Polyunsaturated fatty acids such as omega 3 and omega 6 are essential for the smooth running of our brain. We rarely lack omega 6, present in meat, cereals, sunflower oil, but we are often deficient in omega 3. These are found in fatty fish (sardines, seafood, salmon) but also in spinach, rapeseed or walnut oil. It may be wise to take omega 3 supplements. Research has established the link between omega 3 intake from food and an improved ability to make decisions, get organized and stay focused[10].

The brain is also fond of vitamins - in particular those of the B group – necessary for the production of hormones such as serotonin and dopamine. A good level of vitamin B12 (found in eggs, liver, sardines, seaweed and bananas) is associated with brain plasticity, i.e. the ability of our brain cells to create new connections between them. Vitamin D is also essential: it supports the hippocampus, involved in learning and memory.

Finally, note the importance of iron, essential to transport oxygen to the brain. Iron is present in meat and any vegetable alternative such as lentils and, when associated with vitamin C, is assimilated more efficiently. Lack of energy is sometimes the indicator of an iron deficiency, anemia, particularly prevalent in women.

In recent years, the link between nutrition and psychiatry has been better established. The activity of the hippocampus, a brain area that plays a role in mental health, depends on external stimuli, including food. Scientific evidence[11] suggests that a healthy diet helps reduce the risk of (or treat) mental health problems such as depression or anxiety disorders. The correlation between diet and mental health has been established across all age groups. With anxiety problems on the rise, especially among young people, is it not urgent to raise awareness of the benefits of a healthy diet not only for physical well-being, but also for mental health? Some managers

---

10 Harvard Health Letter, "Do omega-3s protect your thinking skills?", Harvard Health Publishing (2016).

11 F.N. JACKA, O'NEIL, et al, "A randomised controlled trial of dietary improvement for adults with major depression," BMC Med, Vol.15 (2017).

have realized this and are promoting healthy eating in the workplace – for example, by providing healthy snacks instead of pastries and other sweets in meeting rooms.

What if sleep were the key to your vitality?

How about a miracle drug that increases your physical energy while enhancing your well-being, supports your immune system while strengthening your memory, raises your ability to concentrate while stimulating your creativity, ensures emotional regulation while reducing the risk of anxiety, is beneficial to each of your organs while ensuring the optimal functioning of your biological functions? This "medicine" exists. It is entirely natural and is called "restorative sleep"!

Sleep is presumably the most crucial, and unfortunately often discounted, source of energy in a busy work life. Neuroscientist Matthew Walker[12] humorously and provocatively suggests that sleep is the most powerful performance-enhancing drug that people neglect the most. While many aspects of sleep are still mysterious, scientific advances in recent years have revealed benefits that probably go beyond your imagination.

Question of quantity

All animals need rest at one time or another - some more than others. The giraffe, for example, gets less than two hours of sleep per day. Elephants and horses also sleep very little, with two to three hours per day. At the other end of the spectrum is the bat, which sleeps nearly twenty hours a day[13]!

Of all living species, humans are the only ones who intentionally postpone falling asleep. And this is precisely what generates sleep debt. Lack of sleep is a modern-day evil that inexorably

---

12 M. WALKER, *Why we sleep*, Scribner (2018).

13 Dr. R. HEINZER, J. HABA-RUBIO, *Je rêve de dormir*, Favre (2016).

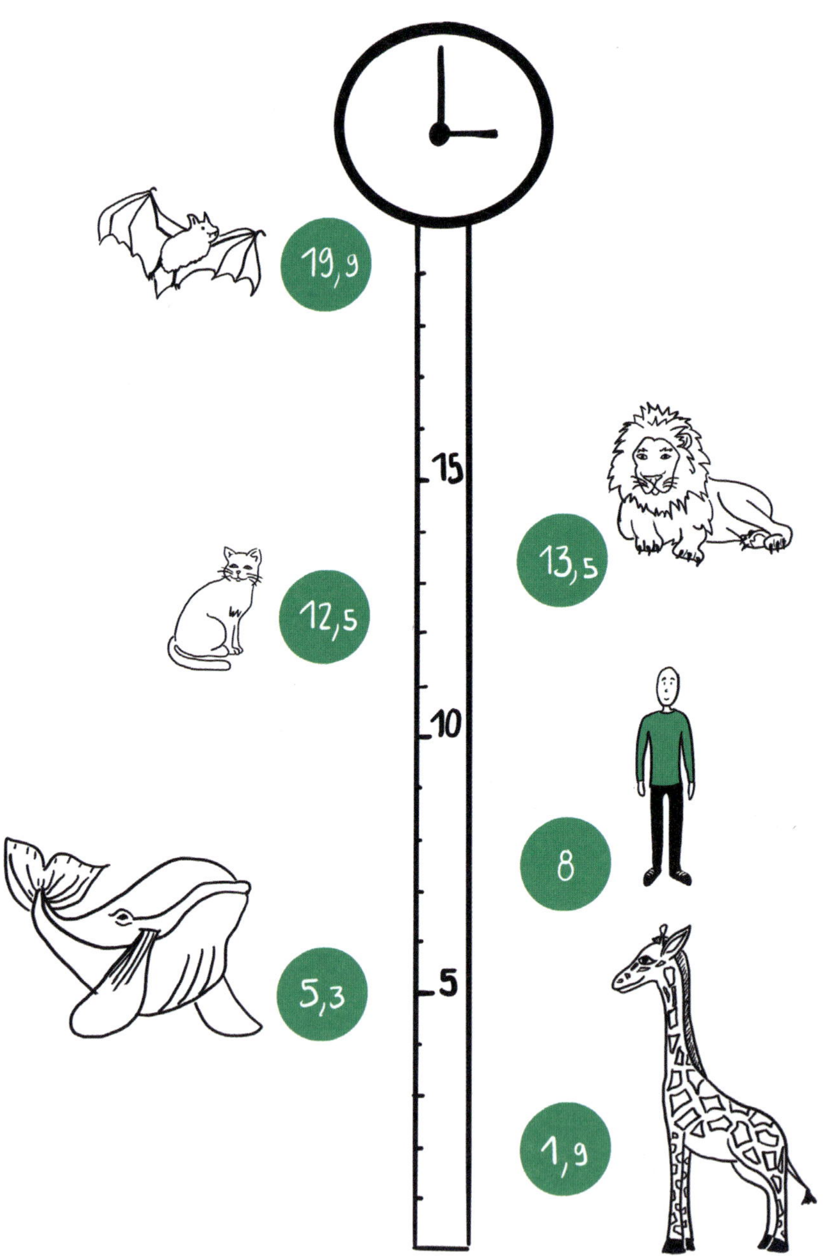
19,9
15
13,5
12,5
10
8
5,3
5
1,9

affects our connected civilization. On average, we sleep 1.5 hours less than fifty years ago. People sleep the least in Japan, with a sleep duration of only 5 hours and 59 minutes. The longest sleep period is recorded in New Zealand, with 7.5 hours[14]. The French sleep on average of 6 hours and 42 minutes each night, below the recommended minimum 7 hours, according to a study by *Santé Publique France*[15]. Too little sleep can seriously impair cognitive abilities. Compounding the problem is the tendency for tired people not to notice their situation and overestimate their performance.

Research suggests that one out of three persons suffers from sleep disorders. The almost constant presence of light - especially that emitted by screens – stress, sedentary lifestyles, but also poor diets, are the main reasons for this disrupted sleep in our modern societies.

At cause, a desynchronized biological clock!

The biological clock is located in our brain, in the suprachiasmatic nucleus of the hypothalamus. It is a set of neurons that, like a conductor, give the rhythm to a number of biological actions of the body. Cortisol, for example, giving us the morning boost to get up, is secreted in the early hours and not at night. The body temperature drops at night and not during the day. Appropriate daylight exposure coupled with darkness at night allow for an optimal synchronization of the biological clock. All animal and plant species have their own internal clock, set to their own rhythm. In humans, the essential synchronizers of our biological clock are melatonin (a sleep-inducing hormone) and light.

---

14 www.sleepcycle.com

15 D. LÉGER, F. BOURDILLON, "The decline in sleep time in France is not a fatality," Santé Publique France (2019).

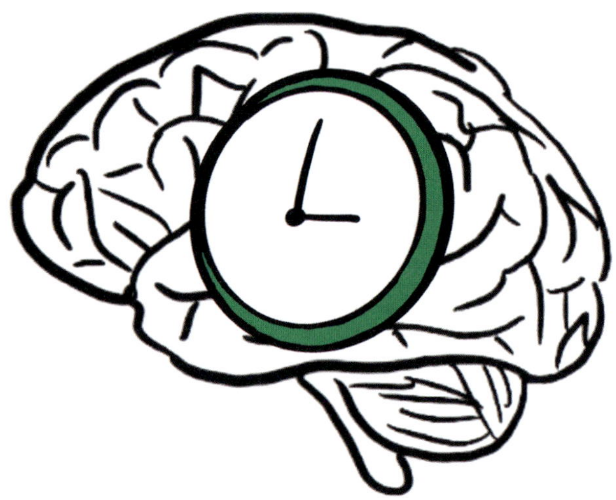

Sleep is not an unproductive period; on the contrary, it is a period during which the brain can regenerate itself, assimilate the impressions of the day and create new connections. Need for sleep is specific to each individual. As a general rule, an adult (aged 18 to 65) needs 7 to 8 hours of sleep per night to function optimally.

Bedtime has the highest influence on the duration of sleep since wake-up time is generally quite stable. Going to sleep earlier is the simplest and most effective recommendation to get more sleep. However, regulating your wake-up time is often the first advice given by sleep experts. Waking time acts as a metabolic trigger. When you wake up at the same time every day (weekends included), you synchronize your biological clock and spare your physiology the negative effects of *social* jet lag; unfortunately, sleeping in on weekends gives an illusion of recovery... Except in cases of extreme fatigue, it is not recommended. By sleeping in, your body operates the necessary adjustments to be in phase with this new, albeit artificial, time zone, along the homeostasis mechanism. It is akin to spending every weekend in New York, while residing in Paris during the week. Imagine the negative consequence on your energy level!

A matter of quality

Sleep is a succession of 3 to 6 cycles of 60 to 120 minutes each. Each cycle in turn is composed of alternating phases of sleep, corresponding to different brain activity levels - as measured by an electroencephalogram (EEG).

A phase of progressively deeper sleep follows the light sleep phase, just after falling asleep. During REM (*Rapid Eye Movement*) sleep, the brain activity is close to that of the waking phase. This phase is called "REM" because of the rapid eye movements (under closed eyelids) observed during this period. It is the period with the highest dream activity.

During any given night, the first cycles are in deep sleep, while the end of the night gives way to REM sleep. Sleep quality is very dependent on the presence of melatonin. In adults, this sleep-inducing hormone is usually released around 21.00 hours. About 90 minutes later, signals of fatigue are felt. If you go to sleep well after the release of melatonin, the amount of deep sleep is affected. It has been proven that the blue light emitted by screens (television, computer, smartphone) is perceived by our brain as an alertness signal. Matthew Walker, in his book *Why we sleep*, purports that one hour on a screen postpones the peak release or melatonin by three hours. This makes it harder to fall asleep. The amount of deep sleep, affected by the reduced amount of melatonin, is lower, which in turn influences the quality of your night.

Unsurprisingly, sleep needs vary from one person to another and over the course of a lifetime, in quantity as well as in quality. Genetic factors can explain the *early riser* or *late sleeper* type.

The circadian physiological cycle (on average a bit over 24 hours) would be somewhat longer for the *late sleeper*. Environment, lifestyle, and life pattern play a key role in our ability to enjoy a restful sleep.

In simple terms, remember that deep sleep – especially in the early part of the night – is the time when you recover physically. During this phase you release the largest amount of growth hormones, essential for strengthening your immune system, and of testosterone, which acts as an antidote to stress. REM sleep, on the other hand, seems to be essential for memory, creativity and the regulation of your emotions. Lack of sleep, thus also lack of REM sleep, is one of the reasons explaining the *post-traumatic stress symptoms (PTSS)* suffered by soldiers after they return from combat zones. Deprived of sleep during their missions, they are also deprived of this natural tool of emotional regulation.

Bring your attention to the present moment and ask yourself these few questions:

- Does my daily routine promote calm and vitality?
- Have I scheduled time in my calendar for physical exercise?
- What meetings during the week could I turn into stand-up or walking meetings?
- Do my eating habits serve me?
- What could I adjust in my current regimen to sustain my energy and focus?
- When I wake up feeling fit and rested, what has been my amount of sleep?
- What is my bedtime routine?

To conclude this chapter, I would like to emphasize how a healthy relationship with oneself represents the basis for establishing healthy relationships with others. Knowing one´s strengths and weaknesses allows for an access to others with increased humanity and tolerance.

Identifying and managing your personal resources attentively bolsters personal resilience, an imperative condition for building team resilience. I regret that our educational systems still leave so little room for this self-discovery process. Let us hope that today´s challenges encourage the education sector to realign priorities and integrate personal development into school programs.

Ready to take action? Go to page 149 to make your selection from the *Practical Menu*.

CHAPTER 3

RELATION WITH OTHERS

> *"People will forget what you said, people will forget what you did, but people will never forget how you made them feel."*
>
> **Maya Angelou**

Every interaction counts. Every interaction is an opportunity to increase employee motivation and confidence... or conversely, to decrease engagement and enthusiasm.

It seems to me that building quality relationships within your staff, but also with all the stakeholders of a project, is the *sine qua non* condition to lead a team with benevolence and success. I have made the observation in different environments – my local grocery store, my children's school, restaurants, organizations where I have worked as a consultant – how those who take care of their relationship with the other have the greatest impact.

Whether you have recently been promoted to a managerial position, or have been leading a team for years, you most likely aspire to showcase your best self; to demonstrate what makes you a *good leader* – assertive, decisive, inspiring, and confident – so as to have more impact on your team. But what about your dark side, your limitations, your weaknesses... all the elements that do not make you a *good leader* in the narrow sense? May the answer be to develop authentic leadership?

Impact and authenticity

The principle of authenticity is not new; since antiquity, authenticity has been considered a virtue by which an individual expresses who he is deep inside, with sincerity. However, associating authenticity with leadership is more recent. The development of positive psychology in the 90's has favored the awareness of appropriate behaviors, rather than pointing the dysfunctional ones. With this backdrop, the concept of authentic leadership has spread in recent years. Many books encourage managers to show themselves *as they truly are*.

Bill Georges, professor at Harvard Business School, former CEO of Medtronic, and author of several best-sellers, proposes 5 dimensions that support authentic leadership: meaning, values, heart, relationships, and self-discipline.

Although several theories exist on the subject, I focus on 3 key characteristics of the authentic leader:

The authentic leader knows himself well and is not afraid of regular introspection.

We emphasized the importance of self-awareness in the previous chapter. We mean holistic self-knowledge, which obviously includes awareness of your strengths and limitations, knowledge of your body, your emotions, and your aspirations. It includes having gone through a personal process aimed at understanding how your own history, and life experience, have shaped the person you are today. An authentic leader reveals the same personality in public and in private. He does not have to put on a costume when leading his team, because he is totally in tune with his true nature. He does not need to hide his mistakes or weaknesses, acts instead with honesty and transparency. Being transparent does not imply unfiltered speaking and acting; it means respecting one´s own limits, those of others and creating trust. American author Brené Brown[16] talks about the *power of vulnerability* as the courage to face risk and show one´s emotions. It is not about revealing everything about yourself without restraint, but about sharing what is appropriate, with humility. Admitting mistakes and learning from them is an example of authentic leadership. Consider Eric Yuan, CEO of the video conferencing platform Zoom: while his company was experiencing tremendous growth at the onset of the Covid-19 pandemic, flaws in IT security and privacy emerged. Eric Yuan publicly apologized to users via a YouTube video (posted on April 8, 2020), acknowledging that he had been too quick to seize growth opportunities, and pledged to remedy the situation by taking swift action. More recently, German Chancellor Angela Merkel acknowledged in a press conference (March 24, 2021) that her decision to lock down the country for five days around Easter weekend was a *personal mistake* – "mistakes must be mentioned by their names" she added. In both cases, the leader´s attitude is a demonstration of humility, while maintaining the assertiveness needed to deal with a critical situation. Is admitting a mistake a confession to weakness or a way to strengthen your impact? My colleague at the Resilience Institute in Australia, Stuart Taylor, talks about *asser-*

---

16 B. BROWN, *Dare to lead*, Penguin Random House (2018). 17 S. TAYLOR, Assertive humility, Monterey Press (2013).

tive humility[17]. When you are able to humbly acknowledge a professional mistake, you foster a culture of transparency. When you share this experience and learn from it, you personify a constructive attitude, the basis of the *growth mindset*[18] which enables individual and collective growth. Recognizing your responsibility as a leader is also beneficial for the entire company. A large American study[19], conducted over a period of eighteen years, has shown that when a leader attributes negative results to external causes, the stock price tends to fall. On the other hand, when he points to internal sources and offers solutions, the value of his company's shares increases because confidence is restored. Despite the scientific evidence supporting the benefits of such a practice, situations of managers acknowledging a mistake and apologizing are still the exception.

The authentic leader acts with his head and with his heart.

He takes care of the relationship. He is not afraid to show his emotions or vulnerability as long as he is in line with reality. An authentic leader is not *soft* or *fragile*. **On the contrary, his attitude is a sign of self-confidence – the audacity to be one true self in order to better serve others**. As mentioned earlier, it is not about being naked and revealing everything about yourself. I do not think it is appropriate or constructive to share all your feelings with your team. The authentic leader finds the right attitude, with discernment – acting with his head and with his heart. New Zealand's Prime Minister Jacinda

---

17 S. TAYLOR, *Assertive humility*, Monterey Press (2013).

18 C. S. DWECK, *Mindset*, Little Brown Book Club (2017).

19 G.R. SALANICK, J.R. MEINDL, "Corporate attributions as strategic illusions of management control", *Administrative Science Quarterly*, vol. 29, n°2, pp238-254, Sage Publications (1984).

Ardern incarnates an excellent example. She responded to the tragic terrorist attacks in Christchurch (March 15, 2019) with immense empathy. With her heart, she was able to create great closeness with her people.

The authentic leader is motivated by a mission beyond himself and takes a long-term perspective.

He pursues goals beyond self-interest, personal financial gain, or ego. In this manner, he prompts decisions that are motivated by what feels "right" and is in line with the organization's purpose. In large companies, especially listed ones, short term tyranny often dominates; decisions are made with a narrow focus and exclusively serve the interest of shareholders. This is unsustainable and completely contrary to the notion of authentic leadership. We shall return to this point in Chapter 5.

Several studies have demonstrated the benefits of authentic leadership. For example, one study[20] found that authentic leadership is the best predictor of employee satisfaction, engagement, and happiness at work. Another[21] found that the perception of a more authentic leader stimulates innovation and employee initiative. Finally, and more recently, a large study by the *Harvard Business Review*[22] points out that leaders' authenticity increases their effectiveness and adhesion of employees.

---

20 S.M. JENSEN, F. LUTHANS, "Entrepreneurs as authentic leaders: impact on employee's attitudes", Leadership & Organisation Journal (2006).

21 M. CERNE, M. JAKLIC, M. SKERLAVAI, "Authentic Leadership, Creativity, and Innovation: A Multilevel Perspective," Sage Journal (2013).

22 B. GEORGE, P. SIMS, A. McLEAN. D. MAYER, "Discovering your authentic leadership," HBR (April-May 2020).

The daily relationships you establish give opportunities to live authenticity. These connections occur on several occasions; some are formal, others informal. Every interaction is an opportunity to build a quality relationship: the way you greet your colleagues or co-workers in the morning, your attitude during meetings, breaks, the tone you use in your writing or on the phone, your reaction to unexpected events, etc.

In short, to make an impact within your team, being authentic is the way to go. It requires true intention, active work, total presence, and attention to each other.

One team, one safe space

In 1999, Harvard Business School professor Amy Edmondson used the term *psychological safety* to identify the most successful teams. Her research[23] highlighted the importance of forging a virtual space where team members dare to take risks, freely express their opinions without fear of being rebuked, and can learn from their mistakes. She has observed how psychological safety fosters the desire to learn – the openness, curiosity, and creativity – that sustains team performance.

This desire to learn, for example, is expressed in the regular exchange of feedback within the team, the transparent sharing of information, the ease of talking about one's mistakes with colleagues, and the ease in daring to ask for help from others. It is not about being buddies; indeed, this same research purports that excessive cohesion between team members can lead to avoidance in expressing disagreements

23 A. EDMONDSON, "Psychological safety and learning behaviors in work teams," Administrative Science Quarterly (1999).

or challenging a colleague's ideas. It is precisely avoidance that undermines the risk-taking attitude that is so essential for innovation and learning.

Psychological safety is based on a shared belief that the team is a safe space to take risks and be fully oneself. The workplace thus becomes a place of fulfillment. Yes, you read that correctly: a place of fulfillment, a place where you can be fully yourself. Do not think I am naive or idealistic. Above all, I am pragmatic: self-fulfillment allows the expression and expansion of talents. It's a win-win for both the individual and the team. For you, the leader, being authentic is therefore also a

way to allow others to be authentic. An atmosphere of trust and mutual respect must be created.

Here are 3 practical suggestions, inspired by the work of A. Edmondson, worth considering at your next team meeting:

- Present a challenge as a learning opportunity rather than a problem to be solved.
- Recognize your own flaws.
- Be curious and ask lots of (good) questions; not judgmental questions, but constructive questions that clarify and free up creativity.

A few years after A. Edmondson, in 2015, Google launched the *Aristotle* research project, a large study aimed at uncovering the general principles behind the most successful teams. This investigation confirmed that for a team, psychological safety is the essential element to achieve optimal performance. The focus is on conversational equality and the importance for everyone feeling heard. Practically, the way forward is encouraging people to speak up, especially those who tend to be more reserved. The greatest managers are attentive to this; it requires social sensitivity and the will to forge and consolidate this safe space, on a daily basis.

Bring your attention to the present moment and ask yourself these few questions:

- **When someone on my team makes a mistake, how do I tend to react?**
- **How positively do I welcome opinions that differ from my own?**
- **Does everyone in our team feel comfortable raising issues?**
- **Are we open to differences?**

- Are risk-taking and initiative valued?
- Does everyone dare to ask for help from the others?
- Do I fully value the talents and skills of everyone on the team?

The leader´s presence - attention control and focus

How present are you in meetings? How do you feel when you arrive at work? How do you feel when you attend a meeting where your boss keeps tapping on his phone? How do you feel when your conversation is constantly interrupted by distractions? Embodying leadership is also about showing it with your heart and body.

Defining precisely what presence means is so difficult. Is it the charisma that emanates from a person, his consideration and small gestures for you, or his capacity of concentration, his focus? Presence cannot be measured but can be felt. You can remember shaking hands with a celebrity years later, and the experience you had at that moment. Similarly, a boss arriving at the office in the morning and ignoring everyone demonstrates total lack of interest in his team. Busy schedules demand so much of our attention that, with no special carefulness, the risk of being absent is high, how unlikely it may seem.

Your presence is an integral part of the relationship you build within your team, but also with your customers, colleagues, or shareholders.

Even before speaking, our bodies emit signals of presence... or absence!

We are constantly sending messages. Given the responsibilities you carry, it is like having a spotlight on you all the time, even in a small team.

Of course, physical size plays a role - being 1.95 m increases the impression of presence, compared to a shorter person. However, many great leaders were, or are, not so tall: Napoleon (1.68 m), Nicolas Sarkozy (1.66 m), Angela Merkel (1.65 m) and Kamala Harris (1.61 m) have developed other strategies to make their presence felt. It is better to let go of elements out of your control, and pay attention to what you can influence:

Can you improve your *being there*? I am sure you can! It is a skill like any other. While some people naturally exude more presence, it is possible to develop other components that will complement your intrinsic nature. Some of these components are remarkably visible and tangible while others are much less so.

Included in the visible part are, for example, your well-groomed appearance, appropriate clothing, upright and open posture (avoid a hunched back or hunched shoulders), body language, facial expressions, or tone of voice. Even before starting a conversation, you radiate (or not) presence. While virtual meetings deprive us of certain cues, it is the more important for those cues to be displayed on a screen. Take facial expressions – which appear on video conferencing platforms when in close-up, and are very revealing of a person's degree of presence.

What is invisible is your attention to, and interest in, the other.

This is valid not only during important meetings, or when you are making significant decisions, but in everyday activities. We can define this mindful presence as the ability to live fully in the moment and give the person you are interacting with your entire attention.

Attentive presence sustains a kind of resonance between a leader and his team, a shared feeling of being on the same wavelength. Being present does not come naturally. Unlike other mammals, humans spend a great deal of time thinking about what is not happening right now. They mull over past or future events, and some that will never happen! According to an American study[24], we spend almost half of our waking time (46.7% to be exact) thinking about something other than what we are doing. The major obstacle to being in the moment and controlling your attention is a restless mind; when the flow of thoughts causes you to ruminate about past events or cultivate anxiety about the future. Why did I say this in this meeting? What a bunch of idiots for making this decision! What happens if this project is not approved? What if my client is not satisfied? The list of toxic thoughts that prevent us from being in the moment, and therefore available for each other, is endless...

Continued investigations in this study explored a possible correlation between presence and happiness. The result : people feel less happy when the flow of thoughts drives them away from the present moment.

Lack of attention to the present moment seems to be our default mindset. Our brain's activity, particularly intense during the day, is dependent on the multiple stimuli we are exposed to. Difficulty focusing on a task reduces our productivity in the same way that difficulty paying full attention to a person reduces our presence.

---

24 M.A. KILLINGSWORTH, D.T. GILBERT, "A wandering mind is an unhappy mind," *Science*, vol. 330 / issue 6006, pp. 932 (2010).

Attention can be defined as the ability to select, and focus on, the most important stimuli. In our ultra-connected world, attention is prized and coveted. Yves Citton, in his book *L'économie de l'attention*[25], mentions attention as the basis of a new economic system, on its way to replace the old way of exchanging material goods; attention constitutes the first scarcity and the most precious source of value.

Professional athletes know that total presence is essential to achieve optimal performance. Imagine Roger Federer, in the middle of a match, ruminating about the previous lost point, focusing on the importance of the next point, or checking his smartphone between games. Such an attitude would obviously be detrimental to his performance.

Now think back about your last conversation with a team member: were you really there? Or were you just physically present, but mentally somewhere else? At what point did you decide to focus all your attention on the person? Were you all ears or discreetly checking your email?

The ability to pay attention is of critical importance when managing a team. Luckily, we can improve and train it!

The first step is deciding to focus, choosing to guide your attention to the present moment. Putting the phone away in meetings, turning off a second screen during video conferences, and deleting automatic notifications, are some tricks that contribute to attentiveness. Mindfulness and meditation techniques – whose effectiveness has been scientifically and clearly demonstrated – strengthen the presence muscle. No need to spend several hours a day on it, a few minutes or regular practice (daily, ideally) calm the mind; staying focused and attentive during the day becomes easier with time. Learn-

25 Y. CITTON, *The ecology of attention*, Polity (2016).

ing to tame distractions and calm a restless mind gradually strengthens one's capacity for attentive presence.

The leader's true presence allows for gain of trust by those he interacts with. This goes far beyond charisma or presentation skills. It is the result of intentional attentiveness and focus on the other person. Training attention control and focus also contributes to your personal resilience: the Resilience Institute, which measures resilience of individuals and teams, has demonstrated that the people with the highest resilience scores are also those with the highest focus capacity.

Creating a safe space thus means offering your team the gift of your caring presence and benevolence. It is a decision that not only helps strengthen your impact but also your resilience.

Creating proximity... at a distance

We are fundamentally gregarious beings. Socialization is a well-recognized need, whose importance is explained by several theories. The most famous one is Abraham Maslow's (1908-1970) hierarchy of needs. An American psychologist and philosopher, Maslow suggested in 1947 that psychological health (which is often referred to as *mental health*) depends on the satisfaction of human needs, from the most basic one up to self-actualization. This model, often represented as a pyramid, identifies 5 categories of needs.

In the workplace, being part of a team is insufficient to create a sense of belonging. Remember the last team-building event, festive dinner or Friday team drinks you organized. All these initiatives are aimed at creating that sense of belonging. They often contribute but are rarely enough. You still

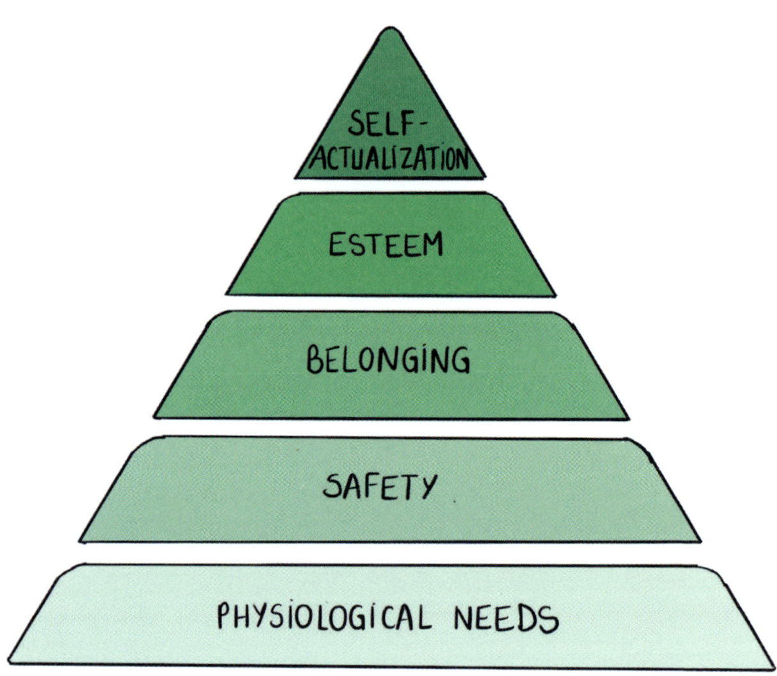

need to ensure smooth communication and establish trustworthy relationships within a team. Can this be what is called proximity? A deep sense of inclusion, a form of *resonance* - that feeling of being on the same page (more on this later when we discuss empathy). A resilient leader works to create this closeness with his employees.

In the telecommuting era, in a world where you can lead a team scattered around the world, how do you meet your staff's need of belonging and proximity? How do you make up for those important moments of togetherness when there is no physical contact? Issues that only increase a leader's challenge.

I often note that geographical distance is compensated by very frequent communication over diverse channels (e-mails, telephone, instant messaging); every group member is in almost permanent connection with his teammates. Inasmuch as frequent communication is useful, constant communication is counterproductive. It can lead to a feeling of being constantly monitored; during the Covid-19 pandemic, many employees complained about the burden of this quasi-continual connection. I recall a bank employee working from home who avoided turning off her computer during breaks, for fear that her boss would suspect her of slacking. Or the teacher whose online classes were recorded for later retrieval by absent students, but who feared that the quality of his teaching would be scrutinized by the school principal.

A resilient leader organizes communication rituals, balanced in quantity and quality. He can, for example, set up formal and informal discussion forums that bring people together without becoming intrusive. It is not an easy balance to strike.

We noted earlier that, according to Amy Edmondson, team cohesion can be an impediment to establishing a *safe space* – one that allows for questioning, sharing of feedback, and frank conversations. So, what to do? Get close... but not too close? Connect... but not too tightly?

To solve this dilemma, I suggest paying attention to the trust you manage to establish with each and every member of your team. In my opinion, reciprocal confidence is at the heart of the sense of belonging to a team.

Looking more closely at the variables of trust[26], four elements are at play:

- The skills you identify in the other person
- The integrity and the coherence between what is said, thought and done
- The benevolence and the care a person demonstrates to another person
- The affinities, similarities, and chemistry between the people

The first two elements are of cognitive nature and can be rationally evaluated by observing behaviors and attitudes. The next two are emotions- and feelings-based. In order to nurture a feeling of trust within a team, you can decide to cultivate these last two elements in a very concrete way, even remotely. Demonstrate that you care about each person, take an interest in them beyond their professional role, identify and highlight what you have in common with them. This simple suggestion is a remarkably quick way to create closeness. Revealing something you have in common with another person (a passion for cycling, having lived in China, being the parent of twins or any other common ground), naturally brings people closer.

Bring your attention to the present moment and ask yourself these few questions:

- **How can I build team cohesion without overdoing it?**
- **Is there fluid communication within the team ?**
- **What team rituals bring us together?**

---

26 O. MESLY, "Faisabilité de Projets", Presses Internationales Polytechniques de Montréal (2015)

- **With whom in the team is my relationship a little less easy?**
- **What do I have in common with this person?**
- **How can I show her care while being authentic?**

Empathy and compassion at work

Creating proximity obviously requires some kind of empathy. During the 20th century, the word was virtually inexistent in management manuals. Empathy can no longer be ignored (it is featured on the cover of many leadership manuals) since the awareness of the importance of emotional skills, their impact on performance and the appreciation of emotional intelligence.

Some people may be more empathetic than others (total absence of empathy is extremely rare and pathological), but it is also a competence that can be developed. Empathy is a form of comprehension: appreciating or acknowledging the emotions of others. Activating empathy – how do I deal with my observation of the other person's emotions – is a demonstration of your emotional intelligence. Some bosses have a lot of empathy but misuse it to manipulate their entourage or – even worse – to look down on others.

In the extreme, one can argue that the greatest manipulators are endowed with a significant deal of empathy. They use this information for political or nefarious purposes.

The good news is that on the empathy front, progress is within reach. You just need to apply the following 4 skills :

1. Listen carefully

Your total presence is required (see above). Pretending to master this competence if you are constantly on your phone during meetings is meaningless. You should focus your full attention on the person and encourage information sharing by asking open-ended questions.

2. Read non verbal cues

It is common knowledge that words are only a marginal part of language, despite the open debate about the exact share of non-verbal communication. Deciphering non-verbal cues such as gestures, facial expression, tone of voice, and breathing rhythm allows for the refinement of our perception of the emotion felt by the other person. Paul Ekman[27], an American psychologist, is a pioneer in the study of emotions and their link to facial expressions – in particular, micro-expressions that last only 1/25th of a second. His research led him to conclude that facial expressions are a universal system of signals that reflect fluctuations in a person's emotional state, moment by moment. Training to detect these signals more accurately will enhance your capacity to feel empathy.

3. Acknowledge the other's perspective

We have shown above how of welcoming and valuing different opinions is a competence, and helpful in forging a safe space. It is also a skill in empathy. By re-stating "what I hear you saying is this...?", "is this correct?", "did I understand your point of view to be...?", you identify different feelings and opinions.

---

27 www.paulekman.com

4. Understand the other's perspective

When you admit a distinct perspective, you do not necessarily convey your understanding of it. Utterly understanding people (without agreeing) means that you have *put yourself in their shoes*. Given what you know about the person, you understand how he comes to his perspective. Achieving this level of competence is the result of serious personal development work.

Personal note: I still have a long way to go on the path to empathy to reach this ultimate level!

When your empathy grows, it gives you access to new knowledge and an improved understanding of your team to better guide it.

Compassion at work is about activating empathy with respect and kindness.

The etymology of this word (from the Latin: *cum patior* "I suffer with" and the Greek: *sym patheia* "sympathy") does not quite make my point. Compassion is, however, a feeling that induces the perception of the suffering of others and the drive to remedy it.

Actually, the question is not about suffering to help others. The issue is not about carrying other peoples' misery as it can lead to empathic distress, an emotional exhaustion that health professionals, educators, or other professionals emotionally (and often also physically) involved can feel.

Compassion implies caring for the other with the intention of relieving them of their pain, alleviating their suffering.

Imagine for a moment a surgeon about to perform an operation. The patient's facial expression leaves no doubt that he feels apprehension. With empathy, the surgeon acknowledges the emotion of fear and turns to the patient: "You are terrified. I understand you. I am not very comfortable either, but hopefully everything goes well." This attitude will obviously not relieve the patient, on the contrary! Suppose the surgeon gives a different answer: "You are scared. I can see that. Don't worry, I've performed this operation many, many times. Everything is going to be fine, and I'll see you when you wake up."

Now imagine the unfortunately realistic scenario: you have to let go someone, probably the most dreaded part of their role for most managers. Once the decision has been made, what will make the difference is how you communicate it and how you support the person in the following days.

I recall the story of a manager who was fired on a Monday morning, on the spot, for reasons of *strategic divergence*. He barely had time to pack his things and say goodbye to his colleagues. Zero compassion. Fortunately, most termination situations are handled humanely and by people who choose to activate their empathy in a positive and constructive way. Demonstrating compassion requires patience, wisdom, and personal resilience.

Research in neuroscience[28] has shown that empathy and compassion activate different areas of the brain. Empathy creates a form of emotional resonance: I share the emotion I am witnessing, and my brain gets in tune. If it is joy, the neural circuitry activated is the one linked to positive emotions. When faced with the suffering of another person (the patient terrorized before surgery or the employee being dismissed), empathy kicks in, inviting us to feel the emotions of the other person. Empathy precisely affects the area of the brain linked to suffering. Sharing the other person's pain therefore activates the same neural circuit in the brain

---

28 T. SINGER, O. KLIMECKI, "Empathy & Compassion," Current Biology. vol. 24. R875-R878 (2014).

as the person suffering. This can lead to emotional contagion or empathic distress if the distinction between self and other is not clearly established. Conversely, the experience of compassion – characterized by a strong motivation to relieve the other, to send love or affection – stimulates the neural circuits linked to positive emotions. Even more fascinating: given the brain's malleability, compassion training – especially through loving *kindness* meditation – not only supports a form of altruism, a more marked attention to the other, but also reinforces resilience and therefore the ability to deal with tricky situations. Empathic response is therefore a necessary step in understanding the emotions at play, but your ability to transform this empathy into compassion makes all the difference.

Talking about love may be surprising in a book on leadership, because kindness and benevolence do not always have good press in a competitive world. However, caring for others is the basis of progress in all collective projects. Cultivating empathy and compassion within your team is therefore a success engine.

The posture of the leader-coach

When I started my professional career, my perception of the boss was tinged with ideals, naivety no doubt, and hope, certainly. It seemed obvious to me that my boss would be the person having the answers to all questions and would provide the solutions to all challenges. All visible and invisible cues supported this expectation of the *expert manager*: a very hierarchical structure, an ultra-codified office layout (a manager had earned the right to occupy his own office, with a window; the next promotion would give him access to a second window); a decision-making process checked by stages and signatures, up to the highly coveted one of the expert bosses, and finally, a promotion system that valued each year of experience as a step to the next stage. This was in 1993, a time when cell phones did not exist, a time when we sent faxes, used a computerized messaging system via an internal network (intranet) but communicated mainly by leaving numerous handwritten notes on desks. Let us remember that Tim Berners-Lee, an English computer scientist, developed the *Worldwide Web* in 1990, the first Internet browser, which was to revolutionize all areas of our lives.

Nearly thirty years later, it is obvious that our ultra-connected world and globalized economy have fundamentally changed the perception of what being a boss means. The posture of the *expert manager* does not stand up to today's reality. A reality summarized by the acronym VUCA *(volatile, uncertain, complex, ambiguous)* that calls for great humility (as highlighted in the first chapter). You most certainly have your own leadership style: the way you motivate, guide, and lead your team. Many authors have proposed diverse ways to identify leadership styles.

The theory of situational leadership was proposed in 1969 by Paul Hersey, an American economist, and Kenneth Blanchard, an American author specializing in management[29]. It rests on the basic assumption that the best leaders adapt their style to the situation, the context, and the person they are dealing with. Hersey and Blanchard describe four main leadership styles: directive, persuasive, participative and delega-

29 P. HERSEY, K.H. BLANCHARD, "Management of organizational behavior", New Jersey/Prentice Hall (1969).

tive. Forty years of research and experience led Blanchard to replace the *persuasive* and *participative* styles with *supportive* and *coaching*. His model encourages identifying the employee´s level of maturity and capacity for a specific task in order to adjust the degree of direction and support he needs. Depending on the situation, your behavior can be directive, coaching, supportive or delegative.

For example, if you have just hired an apprentice to complete your team, you must give clear and specific directions. Your degree of supervision is tighter to ensure that this newcomer understands your goals and expectations. When you interact with someone you have worked with for ten years, your guidance will be quite different, and you will delegate more.

Inspired by this *adaptive* model, in the early 2000´s, Daniel Goleman[30] identified six leadership styles with specific behavioral characteristics:

- **Commanding:** the manager dictates what to do and how to do it.
- **Pacesetting:** the manager sets the tone and an example of high-performance level. He expects the same standard from his team.
- **Visionary:** the manager federates people around an inspiring vision; he shows the why, the meaning, the course.
- **Affiliative:** the manager seeks to create cohesion; he encourages interaction.
- **Democratic:** the manager looks for consensus through democratic means, convinced of the collective intelligence.

30 D. GOLEMAN, R. BOYATZIS, A. McKEE, *Primal leadership*, Harvard Business School Press (2002).

COMMANDING

PACESETTING

VISIONARY

AFFILIATIVE

DEMOCRATIC

COACHING

- **Coaching:** the manager invests in people and aims above all at developing them; he pursues each employee's autonomy and the construction of competent teams.

We must specify from the outset that this list of styles is neither exhaustive nor exclusive.

A good leader will tend to apply several styles to better adapt to the situation and the people he is dealing with.

The word *style* used to define these different theories implies that you can change your approach as you change your clothes, depending on the circumstances, and behave accordingly. By being more alert and proactive, you can develop multiple leadership styles. While remaining true to your natural *self*, having access to a wider range of approaches allows for acting with greater awareness.

Bring your attention to the present moment and ask yourself these few questions:

- **What style do I use naturally?**
- **Is it suitable for everyone in my team?**
- **What style could I reinforce?**
- **What behavior will allow me to use this style more often?**

In Chapter 5 we discuss the question of meaning and come back to the visionary style. This approach is essential in uncertain times when turmoil is likely to sap the motivation and commitment of your employees.

To the word style, I prefer the notion of *posture*. I may be influenced by my yoga practice. In yoga, the concept of posture (*asana* in Sanskrit) is central, all the while being complementary to other dimensions (breathing, meditation, etc.). Some yoga postures seem completely inaccessible until you realize – movement by movement – that you can get close. I like to remind my yoga students that it is not so much the final posture that is so beneficial as the set of movements that lead to the final posture. This brings us back to our subject.

Each of your behaviors, your choices, your decisions define your managerial *posture*. Your employees' perception of you is formed step by step, one interaction after the other.

The current trend in organizations clearly tends to the development of the posture of the leader-coach, although the directive style may be the most appropriate option in exceptional circumstances, or during major crises. Whether you are the owner of your restaurant or the general manager of a multinational company, it is important to adopt an attitude emphasizing your employees' strengths, to support them in their development, to put them in a position to succeed. The leader-coach is benevolent and demanding, favoring constructive dialogue, he masters active listening and the art of giving constructive feedback. The leader-coach invests time in the relationship; he seeks to bring out the best in his co-workers. He assists them on the path towards their objectives, without deciding for them. You are encouraged to play the facilitator role more often, without denying your decision-making responsibility. One of the key skills of the leader-coach style is to ask questions – many, relevant and effective questions.

The art of the leader-coach is to ask the right question at the right time.

Close-ended questions elicit predefined answers, which tends to refocus a conversation, and can be useful in helping to identify the most valuable information.

When faced with an employee overwhelmed by his workload, closed questions help the employee identify more immediate solutions:

- Is project A, B or C the priority this week?
- Do you have time slots during which you disconnect from your email and can be fully focused?
- Do you feel rather overwhelmed or tired?

Open-ended questions broaden the scope of exploration; they are used to gain a deeper understanding, to dig further, to ease the conversation. Open-ended questions typically begin with an adverb or an interrogative adjective/pronoun: What, Who, Where, When, How, Why.

- How do you prioritize your tasks for the week?
- What prevents you from delegating more?
- What are your options in this situation?

And finally, there are those famous *powerful questions* : the ones that bring your counterpart to a turning point, trigger a change of perspective, point the other person to a solution to an issue or simply renew his motivation; you have so successfully adopted the posture of a leader-coach.

- If plan A is not possible, what else is possible?
- How will you feel when you reach this goal?
- What would be the worst-case scenario?
- Is there another solution that is not immediately obvious?
- What do you learn from this experience?

Beware: a good question asked at the wrong time will lose its power. This is the reason why developing empathy is the prelude to adopting the posture of a leader-coach.

Generating enthusiasm and confidence in turbulent times

> *"It is in the nature of all enthusiasm to be communicated and to increase by the number of enthusiasts"*
>
> **Denis Diderot**[31]

Wonder, intoxication, vehemence, euphoria, fervor, passion, dithyramb, rapture, intoxication, ecstasy, ardor. To these many synonyms, I have always preferred the word *enthusiasm*. The Merriam-Webster dictionary defines enthusiasm as *strong excitement* of feeling and *something inspiring zeal or fervor*.

For an ancient Greek, the term alludes to the divine *in-theos*, having a god *within oneself*. The poet, the oracle or the prophet would be inhabited by a force beyond him. While leaving it to each reader to validate this divine connotation, I am particularly sensitive to this old meaning, and the idea of an enthusiasm that is always a surpassing of oneself, a kind of radiant fervor.

A contemporary of Diderot (1713-1784), Voltaire (1694-1778) stated that *nothing is done without a little enthusiasm*. Making decisions is part of your daily life as a leader. Do you have the required enthusiasm to generate commitment from all stakeholders and unite your team? Does this inner fire radiate? Do you give off contagious *positive vibrations*?

We all have memories of intense, positive, collective emotions: attending a soccer game, a concert, sporting events. This collective enthusiasm is multiplied by the number of enthusiasts, as Diderot suggested.

---

31 D. DIDEROT, *Lettre sur les sourds et muets*, Œuvres t. II. P. 373 in Pougens (1751).

We speak of emotional contagion[32]. Christophe Haag, a researcher in social psychology and professor at Emlyon Business School, goes as far as comparing this phenomenon to a virus that acts in a few milliseconds. During a meeting or a discussion, one tends to adopt the facial expressions, the tone of voice, and the posture of the other person, unconsciously and automatically. This reality of unconscious and automatic mimicry is linked to the presence in our brain *of mirror neurons* that stimulate the same body expressions as the interlocutor and will therefore tend to generate the same emotion.

The unwelcome news is that emotional contagion is more effective when it comes to negative emotions, which become more entrenched. As mentioned by American psychologist Rick Hanson, the brain acts on negative emotions like *Velcro* and on positive emotions like *Teflon*.

Mobile technologies and hyper-connectivity bring us live the dramas of this world. You must therefore understand the need to counterbalance this *overflow* of negative emotions within your team.

Triggering positive emotional contagion is a responsibility of the resilient leader.

Not only to preserve or restore an enthusiastic work atmosphere, but also – quite simply – to achieve greater performance. Spinoza (1632-1677) defines emotions – affects as he calls them – as states of the body that increase or decrease its own capacity for action. He argues that joy signals the passage of man from a lesser to a greater perfection. He presents joy as a force of expansion. It is not a matter of fleeting happiness but of an inner state to be cultivated. What is true on a personal level is equally true collectively. Your ability to

32 C. HAAG, *La contagion émotionnelle*, ed. Albin Michel (2019).

generate enthusiasm, even, or especially, in turbulent times is an energy activator. To fully benefit from positive emotional contagion, enthusiasm must be genuine. In this matter, feigning emotion will certainly not have the expected result.

The ability to keep calm under pressure and maintain a positive energy level – your base camp – is the fertile ground for your enthusiasm to flourish. Cultivating your deep and sincere inner joy is the best way to achieve enthusiasm within your team. This raises the question of the conditions of your inner joy – the one that depends less on external factors (others, conditions, context) but more on internal factors (awareness, gratitude, calm). This type of enthusiasm is the most contagious, the most beneficial and the most impactful. Awareness of the conditions that favor the emergence of joy within your team is also critical. You will quickly understand that simple actions can have a significant impact: celebrating modest successes, steps achieved towards an ambitious goal, setting aside time for informal exchanges, celebrating birthdays, greeting everyone when they arrive at or leave the office, acknowledging efforts and showing gratefulness to the team, etc.

Collective enthusiasm is the feeling that dominates when we live an *optimal experience* together. This expression is inspired by the concept of *flow*, described by the Hungarian-American psychologist Mihaly Csikszentmihalyi[33]. It refers to a deeply satisfying positive state, experienced in full consciousness (in the present moment), and generating joy and creativity. On an individual level, it applies to a violinist playing a complex piece brilliantly after hours and hours of practice or to a victorious sportsman after an intense competition. It also relates to the dominating feeling when you achieve a significant professional goal that you hold dear.

Scientists talk about being *in the zone*. Mihaly Csikszentmihalyi's research with athletes, artists, authors, musicians, or workers like you and me, has demonstrated that such a positive state is not random and can be stimulated. He identifies 4 key factors that create the conditions to be in *flow*:

1. The activity or task is inherently motivating
2. Goals are clear and feedback is immediate
3. Available skills are in line with the challenges at hand
4. Focus is full and on the present moment

When a team leader understands (and puts in place) the conditions fostering the emergence of an *optimal experience* among his employees, commitment, and creativity increase. Collective enthusiasm can lift mountains, such is the power of positive emotions.

---

33 M. CSIKSZENTHMIHALYI, *Flow: the psychology of optimal experience*, Harper Perennial Modern Classics (2008).

Henry Ford (1863-1947) said: "Enthusiasm is the basis of all progress". At a time when social progress is no longer a luxury but an imperative, the resilient leader can unleash this personal and collective enthusiasm, a true engine for progress, even on a road full of obstacles.

Bring your attention to the present moment and ask yourself these few questions:

- What drives / hinders my enthusiasm?
- What elements under my control tend to increase my enthusiasm?
- How can I generate more positive emotions in the team?
- What positive rituals can I institute to counterbalance an anxiety-inducing situation?
- Do I understand what allows every member of my team to live an optimal experience?

Communicating with realistic optimism

A good leader is a good communicator. This is a simplistic definition which underlines the importance for any team leader to communicate constructively (in the right way, at the right time, with the right tone), not only with employees but also with all stakeholders. Communication skills are what sets individualists apart from team players. In individual sports, such as running, no communication skills are required; on the other hand, the ability to communicate *as a team* is a key performance factor in all team sports, such as soccer, field hockey or volleyball.

More effective communication clearly increases the impact of the leader and the performance of the entire team. Earlier, we mentioned verbal and non-verbal signals: your presence contributes greatly to the impact of your communication, beyond the words you use. Generally speaking, a leader's formal communication is scrutinized, commented, and analyzed, probably less so in a small organization, but still. I remember attending year-end meetings at my children's school. At the end of the presentation, the principal's message was the subject of numerous interpretations and observations by parents and teachers. No need to remind you of the stakes at play when the CEO of a publicly traded company makes official statements. In such moments, the leader's messages influences and affects employees, but also customers, strategic partners, shareholders, and the media. Effective communication is thus an essential leadership skill.

Thierry Geerts, the head of Google Belgium since 2011, shared in an interview[34] that, naturally shy, he would never have reached this level of responsibility had he not taken acting classes in his youth. He has grasped how vital communication is to a leader who is heard, and therefore followed, by feeling his impact on the audience.

No team, large or small, operates in a closed system. Over the past thirty years, the pace of change has accelerated. The integration of innovative technologies has become widespread in all sectors. A global crisis, like the Covid-19 pandemic, is able to bring the world to its knees. In today's global environment, with so much at stake and so many interdependent factors, no one leader can claim to have the answers

---

34 T. GEERTS, M. VOSSEN, "Thank you, it's Monday," podcast of March 30, 2021, NGroup.

to all possible questions. On the other hand, and thanks to collective intelligence, a group of people is likely to bring out highly innovative solutions.

Guiding a team is akin to navigating in the unknown, looking after your crew and keeping a course. Communicating adequately is even more crucial! How to show humility ("I don't know either"), while demonstrating confidence, assertiveness, and optimism? This is not an easy task. The pessimist who sees everything with a gloomy eye runs the serious risk of lowering morale (a typical example of *negative emotional contagion*). The over-optimist, blinded by fear ("I put on my blinkers so as not to face danger or the unknown") or ambition ("nothing and no one will stop me from achieving my goal") is often dangerous because his risk-taking is disproportionate and his decisions disconnected from reality.

What if, on the optimism scale, you developed the ability to communicate with *realistic optimism*?

At the Resilience Institute, *realistic optimism* is the term we use to intelligently combine humility, assertiveness, courage, and ambition. It is about being realistic, and very lucid, about a given situation: acknowledging the difficulties, the unknowns, the obstacles, and sharing them explicitly with the team. All the while, the resilient leader also shares, with his head and heart, his confidence and optimism in order to face the challenges, as a team. This is realistic optimism!

It is interesting to mention that what is most detrimental to resilience is not so much confrontation with difficulties, but fear of the unknown. Those who are highly intolerant of uncertainty are more likely to experience some form of emotional distress than those who are more receptive. For many people, uncertainty goes hand in hand with anxiety. Similarly, people who are anxious by nature tend to be less tolerant of uncertainty. Therefore, talking openly about difficulties within the team is likely to lift the veil on the unknown *(we are not in denial, but rather acknowledge the obstacles)*, and sustain the resilience of the team.

When the team is perceived as a *safe space* by your employees, it is safe for you as well. Psychological safety is also a door-opener for the leader's humility. With authenticity and without losing legitimacy, you can acknowledge your own limitations and be vulnerable to a situation that may be beyond your control. In these moments, collective enthusiasm, nurtured little by little within a team, can support the assertiveness, courage, and optimism necessary to roll up your sleeves, and all together face the challenges that arise.

Ready to take action? Go to page 152 to make your selection from the *Practical Menu*.

CHAPTER 4

RELATION WITH THE ENVIRONMENT

> *"There are only two ways to live your life. One is as though nothing is a miracle. The other is as though everything is a miracle"*
>
> **Albert Einstein**

How can we not marvel at a sunset, the blue of the ocean, a lush forest, a cherry blossom tree in Spring, the majesty of the mountains, the birth of a baby calf, sunflowers turning toward the light, the colors of a hummingbird, the phosphorescent light of fireflies, the ingenuity of ants or the beauty of a butterfly?

We sometimes overlook nature´s miracles, as we are so taken by our modern existence. Preoccupied with our agenda, train schedules, telephone, computer, and sales targets, we tend to forget how extraordinary planet Earth is.

Many astronauts have testified that seeing the Earth from space for the first time made them instantaneously realize of just how small, fragile and precious our planet is. They called this experience the *overview effect*[35] – a cognitive shock, a

35 F. WHITE, "The Overview Effect - Space exploration and human evolution", AIAA (1998).

sudden state of mental clarity, that renders the need to protect this *little blue dot*[36] clear and imperative.

In 2017, a few days before the end of the Proxima mission that took him to the International Space Station for six months, the French astronaut Thomas Pesquet shares his thoughts on the subject: "We need all this technology to get here and understand the simplicity of things: the Earth, the cosmos, life as a whole. It's hard to understand borders, wars and hatred."

What if we paused to reflect on the relationship we cultivate with nature as a leader, living on earth?

The resilient leader is aware of the world's challenges and makes choices with all stakeholders in mind - employees, customers, shareholders and... the environment. How about becoming a change agent? In this chapter, I put forward a state of play so that you can take an informed look at the solutions emerging in the private sector, and I give some examples of companies that are placing environmental issues at the heart of their strategy.

As I researched and wrote this chapter, I felt hope and confidence grow. Better understanding a situation, no matter how troubling, allows for a lucid approach. The resulting clarity allows us to find the courage to make sometimes difficult choices. The many climate initiatives underway fuel my *realistic optimism* (as described in Chapter 3), and I hope yours as well.

36 "Pale Blue Dot" is the name given by American Astronomer Carl Sagan (1934-1996) to a picture of Earth taken on February 14, 1990, from the Voyager 1 space shuttle 1, at a distance of approximately 6 billion kilometers.

What is nature?

Asking this question is not neutral. The Western worldview distinguishes between human beings and human works on the one hand, and nature on the other. In some cultures, the first peoples for example, this concept is inexistent because plants, animals and humans are included in a global sphere[37]. This perspective is far removed from the interpretations of classical Judeo-Christian thought, for which our species, created by God, has no place in nature but above it. Pope Francis' Encyclical Letter, Laudato Si'[38], addressed in June 2015, reconnects with the original biblical message of respect for nature[39]. Dedicated to environmental and social issues, and in general to the safeguarding of what he calls *our Common Home*, the text is based on a systemic vision of the world and calls for the reader to rethink the interactions between human beings, society and the environment. In this encyclical, Pope Francis emphasizes the interdependence between all species and the planet Earth. It is worth noting that St. Francis of Assisi (1181-1226), the inspiration for the name chosen by the Pope, is often considered the *patron saint of ecologists*, defender of nature and friend of animals. This is a pope whose courage and boldness - in a 2000-year-old institution not prone to innovation - is remarkable!

---

37 P. DESCOLA, *Par-delà nature et culture*, Gallimard (2006).

38 Encyclical Letter Laudato Si' by the Holy Father Francis on Safeguarding the Common House, June 2015, available online: https://www.vatican.va/content/francesco/en/encyclicals/documents/papa-francesco_20150524_enciclica-laudato-si.html

39 J. BASTAIRE, "L'exigence écologique chrétienne", Études, vol. tome 403, n°9, pp. 203-211 (2005).

One surmises that in the Neolithic Age, about 10,000 years ago, when people began to settle down to farm the land, the relationship of humans with nature changed profoundly[40]. The hunter-gatherers, our Paleolithic ancestors, lived by hunting, fishing, and gathering. The corollary of nomadism, following herds in their migrations, was a form of asceticism. There was no incentive in accumulating excessive goods or provisions; the criterion of portability was essential. We can therefore assume that Paleolithic societies lived in a respectful relationship with other species and adaptated to their environment. This hypothesis is evidently far remote from the reality of modern society, whose foundations are based on extraction and exploitation, for the benefit of mankind.

This evolutionary vision of the Man-Nature relation includes the word *nature* in its external meaning (everything that is not human and/or human production). It goes without saying that our inner nature, the human nature, is part of this reflection.

Your relation to your inner nature, your personal ecosystem, influences the relationship you entertain with the outer nature.

This is why the chapters on relationship to oneself and relationship to others precede this one. In short, cultivating a healthy relationship with your inner nature tends to promote a healthier relationship with outer nature. And vice versa. Cultivating a relationship with outer nature nurtures a sense of humility, responsibility and gratitude. It's even beneficial to your health. A fascinating study[41] of the medical records of prisoners in a Michigan penitentiary in the 1970s proved that

---

40 J. DELORD, « L'extinction d'espèce : Histoire d'un concept & enjeux éthiques », Publications scientifiques du Muséum (2010).

41 H. FRUMKIN, "Beyond toxicity - human health and the natural environment", *American journal of preventive medicine*, num 20, pp 234-240 (2001).

visual contact with nature was enough to provide positive effects: those who, by coincidence, were locked in a cell with a view of a natural landscape had a 24% lower risk of suffering health problems than those whose window faced a brick wall. Recent scientific advances clearly demonstrate that contact with nature is necessary for our mental health. The Japanese encourage the practice of *shinrin-yoku* (forest bathing), scientifically recognized for its therapeutic effects. We unconsciously find in nature what has allowed our species to survive and evolve for thousands of years. This link with nature is at the origin of the concept of biophilia (from the Greek *bio* meaning "life" and *philia* meaning "who loves"), designating the visceral love of humans for the living.

Has our society's evolution disconnected us from this intimate relation with nature? A highly likely hypothesis.

Connecting while distinguishing

When it comes to representing nature, two depictions dominate and are in opposition: one entirely includes humans in the universe, the other separates man and nature.

Anthropocentrism puts man at the center of the world and considers him segregated from nature. It is a dominant position vis-à-vis nature. Biocentrism is the opposite. The anthropocentric vision, whose excesses are destructive, is opposed to a vision where nature is sacred. Every living being, human or not, deserves respect and consideration. Man is no longer at the top of the hierarchy of living beings but a part of the whole and has no specific place. If every living being is entitled to respect, there would be no reason to choose the side of humans when they are threatened by other species. Biocentrism is anthropocentrism's opposite extreme... and, as is often the case, extreme positions carry with them harmful excesses.

According to philosopher and sociologist Edgar Morin (born in 1921), either perception is a reflection of a form of laziness that aims at simplifying a complex reality. It invites to conceive uniduality[42], which characterizes a simultaneous relation of implication and separation between man and nature. A question of connecting while distinguishing. Here is an arduous mental exercise for the binary mind that tends to dominate in our Western culture. This perspective is closer to Taoism, a current of Chinese thought, which is based on the existence of a principle at the origin of all things (called tao) and a sense of yin-yang balances – at once distinct and connected.

Nicole Huybens[43], psychosociologist, integrates the complex thought of Edgar Morin to approach the relationship between man and nature through an ecocentric vision. Ecocentrism presents a systemic approach that includes species, communities of living beings and ecosystems. This vision is based on the scientific observation that living (biotic) and non-living (a-biotic) elements interact to form a whole that has its own coherence. Protecting biodiversity therefore becomes a priority issue: if one species disappears, the whole ecosystem is off-balance. This imbalance affects us, living beings. By insisting on the interdependence of life forms within a complex whole, Nicole Huybens invites us to respect the laws of nature:

---

42 E. MORIN, La méthode IV. *Les idées : leur habitat, leur vie, leurs mœurs, leur organisation*, Seuil (1991).

43 N. HUYBENS, La forêt boréale, l'éco-conseil et la pensée complexe. *Comprendre les humains et leurs natures pour agir dans la complexité*, Éditions universitaires européennes (2010).

"Contemplating the beauty of the world, thinking of it as a whole and harmonizing human behavior with the laws of nature are the pillars of the ecocentric vision."

The notion of interdependence is also present in the Gaia theory, which examines all the existing interactions within the Earth system. This theory is an evolution of the Gaia hypothesis, put forward in 1970 by the English climatologist James Lovelock (born in 1919) and the American microbiologist Lynn Margulis (1938-2011). According to this controversial hypothesis (also called the geobiochemical hypothesis), the Earth is a dynamic physiological system which includes the biosphere, in which all living beings form a kind of super-organism - called Gaia - that self-regulates its components to promote life. However, this self-regulation capability, which preserves the conditions for life, is jeopardized by global warming. Theories based on the Gaia hypothesis present an alarming prognosis for the future of the biosphere, and therefore for the future of our species.

How to face the planetary environmental crisis? How to accelerate the necessary changes? How to move from awareness to action? And you, what do you do?

Bring your attention to the present moment to ask yourself these questions:

- When was the last time I marveled at nature?
- What feelings dominate when I am in nature?
- Are environmental issues part of my daily thinking?
- Have I ever discussed environmental issues with my team?
- If not, what is holding me back?
- If I have, how has it been perceived by most employees?

Scientific consensus, facts and figures

In the professional world, pragmatism is the order of the day. In my career, I have witnessed how facts - real and verified - are generally the basis for decisions. Let us thus assume that, as a leader, you are receptive to facts, data, and vetted information. Resilience invites lucidity; only by understanding a situation, as accurately as possible, can you decide on a strategy to rebound, change course and find new momentum. So let us open our eyes, not to be overwhelmed by despair or guilt, but on the contrary to take advantage of our influence - small or big - and choose to move in the direction of the future.

The environmental situation is alarming. The scientific consensus leaves little doubt that global warming will have dramatic consequences. The global exploitation and use of natural resources have progressed at an appalling rate since the 1950s; production methods, our lifestyles and more generally our model of society have led to massive global disruptions: global warming, ocean acidification, drop in biodiversity (on land as well as at sea). Back in 2014, the IPCC stated that greenhouse gas emissions generated by economic and population growth are responsible for these climate disruptions.

"It is now 99.9% certain that humans are the primary cause of global warming" concludes a study published in 2018 in the journal *Science*[44]. The latest IPCC[45] report published on August 9, 2021 confirms this: "Human influence on global warming is unequivocal."

---

44 C.Z. ZOU, F. J. WENTZ, S. SOLOMON, G. PALLOTTA, "Human influence on the seasonal cycle of tropospheric temperature", Science, vol.361; n°6399 (2018).

45 IPCC – Intergovernmental Panel on Climate Change.

The increased awareness of this phenomenon no longer leaves room for denial. Yet, there are climate change deniers, and others merely refusing to consider that it is the result of human activities or its harmful consequences. These are the climate skeptics. It is difficult to listen to their populist, egotistical and often simplistic speeches. A recent study[46] on a large

46 Obs'COP 2020: https://www.edf.fr/observatoire-international-climat-resultats/fr/2020

sample (30 countries + 24 000 people interviewed) concludes that 8% of the population does not believe in global warming. Even more worrying: 23% doubt its human causes, hence our responsibility. The study's conclusion: there is an average of 31% climate skeptics in the world, particularly prevalent in the United States, China, Saudi Arabia, Australia and Norway!

In 2015, the Paris Agreement[47] (adopted at COP21, the Paris climate conference) formalized a global response to the threat of climate change; this declaration of intent (not legally binding), signed by more than 195 countries, aims to keep the increase in global temperature by 2100 below 2°C compared to pre-industrial levels, and to continue efforts to limit it to 1.5°C. Half a degree more makes all the difference; it significantly increases the number of climate refugees, deaths, health problems caused by heat, risks of diseases such as malaria and dengue, droughts, heavy rainfall, etc.

Concretely, to achieve this goal, CO2 emissions would have to fall by 45% by 2030. The current trend leads to a warming of more than 3°C by 2100. There is urgency! In September 2020, Chinese President Xi Jinping announced that he was aiming for carbon neutrality by 2060, which means that by that date China should not emit more greenhouse gases than it absorbs, through tree plantations or technologies to capture CO2. Other countries, such as the United Kingdom, Japan or the United States (under the presidency of Joe Biden), but also the European Union, have also committed to achieve carbon neutrality by 2050.

Ursula von der Leyen, President of the European Commission, unveiled in December 2019 Europe's ambitious environmen-

---

47 COP21, «Adoption de l'Accord de Paris, Décision 1/CP.21», Convention cadre des Nations Unies sur les changements climatiques, UNFCCC (2015).

tal plan: *The European Green Deal*, or EGD[48] *(Green Deal for Europe)*, envisions a systemic approach based on economic growth decoupled from resource exploitation. In July 2021, an arsenal of legislative measures was announced, including the end of gasoline-powered cars and a kerosene tax in the aviation sector. The goal is a 55% reduction in greenhouse gases by 2030, and to be the first carbon-neutral continent by 2050. This roadmap sets a course for a sustainable, equitable and inclusive economy.

Decades of economic growth have completely ignored negative externalities (social or environmental impact) and were evaluated along reductive macroeconomic indicators (GNP). The crisis is now twofold: economic gains only benefit a minority and leave too many people behind; all the while the impact of human activities on the climate and biodiversity threatens the survival of our species. More than just a responsible vision, the *Green Deal for Europe* includes a series of operational measures to shift the economy from an extractive to a regenerative one. The action plan is designed to promote a clean and circular economy while restoring biodiversity and reducing pollution. The European Union also provides financial support and technical assistance to help those who will be most affected by the transition to a *green* economy. While acknowledging the flaws or shortcomings of a Europe that we would often like to be stronger and more unified, I applaud this initiative that reveals the best side of this institution. When intelligence and creativity are put at the service of a global cause, hope is revived.

---

48 Obs'COP 2020: Ec.europa.eu/info/strategy/priorities-2019-2024/europe-an-green-deal_fr

Should all these promises be kept, and according to the Climate Action Tracker[49], global warming could be contained to 2.1°C by the end of the century – not far from, but above the objective of the Paris agreements. But what are promises worth in thirty or forty years from now?

The Greta Thunberg generation

In August 2018, a 15-year-old girl convinces her parents of the climate emergency and decides to raise her country's government awareness about the issue. She settles down in front of the country's parliament, and spends her days there brandishing a sign stating *school strike for climate*. Greta Thunberg, a young Swedish girl born in 2003, was unaware at the time that the movement she initiated would grow to a global dimension and mobilize young people all over the world. The *Fridays for Future* – demonstrations organized by young people – are quickly set up, and benefit from an immense media coverage. Greta Thunberg becomes the symbol of a whole generation of young people, aware of the issues at stake and determined to get decision-makers to move.

Invited to meet with many heads of state, speaking at multiple international conferences, including the United Nations Climate Summit in New York in 2019, Greta points the finger at the political leaders's responsibility, who are doing too little in light of the emergency. She calls them to account with a straight face, and a fiery spirit. We remember her fierce look during the intense speech she gave at the United Nations in

49 Climate Action Tracker is an independent scientific analysis that tracks government actions and progress toward achieving the Paris Agreement goals.

New York in 2018: *How dare you?* Greta's direct style and anger at political inaction have earned her as much praise as criticism. Whatever one thinks of it, Greta Thunberg has been the catalyst of an unprecedented awareness, and has stimulated an extraordinary surge of commitment among the youth. The same young people who may be your employees tomorrow. The young people who are tomorrow's leaders, and want a more responsible world. In 2019, *TIME Magazine* voted Greta Thurnberg "Personality of the Year".

From awareness to responsibility, companies in the process

Corporate Social Responsibility, or CSR, refers to the voluntary recognition by corporations of the economic, social, environmental and ethical issues related to their activities. A company practicing CSR aims for a positive impact on society, respect for the environment, while being economically viable. This delicate balance is struck in partnership with its stakeholders, i.e. employees, customers, suppliers and shareholders. The company voluntarily implements good practices; the business model can be questioned to render it compatible with the fight against climate change or sustainable resource management. CSR is a new vision of the role of organizations and their responsibility in society. This approach is increasingly promoted, and even mandatory in certain jurisdictions, although it is optional. For example, in 2019 in France, the *Pacte* law (French acronym for: Action Plan for the Growth and Transformation of Companies) establishes a minimum legal base for the integration of these CSR dimensions in the conduct of business. In April 2021, the European Commission adopted the CSRD (Corporate Sustainability Reporting Directive[50]) proposal, which aims to harmonize CSR reporting over the next few years and extend it to more European companies with a view to facilitating investments based on ESG criteria (Environment, Social, Governance).

With our perspective of unlimited growth, we have reached unprecedented levels of resource extraction, pollution, and waste. The current state of knowledge shows how unsustainable the standard economic model is. Our view of development is flawed because the way we measure it does not take into account the negative impacts of economic activity – the so-called *negative externalities*, such as pollution, soil depletion or the devastating consequences of deforestation. There is no trace in conventional accounting of the cost to the environment (and therefore to society). Take the example of oil: its market price reflects the cost of extraction but does not

---

50 https://ec.europa.eu/info/publications/210421-sustainable-finance-communication_fr#csrd

include the cost of its manufacturing by nature – the millions of years it takes for organic matter to be transformed into oil. The case for a regenerative economy is growing.

The regenerative model, inspired by the observation of living organisms in nature, and guided by the collaboration principle rather than competition, promotes a local economy, an economy of use and a circular economy.

Some examples[51] distinctly illustrate the relevance of an economy of use (also called functional economy). In Europe, for 92% of its life time, a car is parked, thus unused; 31% of food is wasted and office space is occupied 35-50% of the time, even during working hours (note: these statistics were established before the pandemic). The circular economy, on the other hand, aims to reduce, repair, reuse, redistribute and recycle products that are designed with this in mind. Plastic is a good example. Thanks to innovations in cleaning, smart packaging or waste treatment, plastic waste can be drastically reduced, reused or better managed. New movements are emerging, such as *Circular Economy Switzerland*[52], which bring together private companies and political organizations around the common goal of making the economy more circular.

While initiatives to fight global warming are multiplying, discussions around this environmental issue, whose stakes are political, social, economic, technological, sanitary and ethical, are also continuing. Apart from the climate sceptics mentioned above or the uninformed, no one can claim ignorance. Citizen mobilizations and eco-actions are multiplying: waste sorting, turning off unnecessary lights, favoring soft mobil-

---

51 Ellen MACARTHUR Foundation, "Growth within: a circular economy vision for a competitive Europe", SUN, McKinsey & Co (2015).

52 https://circular-economy-switzerland.ch/

ity, buying in bulk to decrease packaging waste, heating judiciously, saving water, etc. This is commendable and necessary, but obviously not sufficient. In this battle, we have to activate the tripartite – political power/citizen power/business power – to accelerate transition.

Businesses can play a leading role in this climate fight. As a leader, you can contribute to this collective effort, whatever your sphere of influence. The professional world, a breeding ground for multiple intelligences and creativity, has an important part to play in this race against time.

An increasing number of companies is making a commitment to become carbon neutral by 2050 – consuming fewer fossil fuels and offsetting what cannot be eliminated. Under the patronage of the United Nations, the *UN Race to Zero*[53] campaign is scientifically monitoring these initiatives stemming, among others, from the business, political (cities, states, regions), financial, and academic worlds. This coalition represents 708 cities, 23 regions, more than 2,000 companies, 127

---

53 UN Race to Zero - https://unfccc.int/climate-action/race-to-zero-campaign

of the largest investors and 571 academic institutions. Collectively, these actors now cover 25% of global CO2 emissions.

When large companies make structural, and structuring, decisions that are positive for the climate, the lines are moving!

The AXA Group, one of the world's leading insurance and asset management companies, is setting an example: in 2019, AXA announced an ambitious climate strategy that includes objectives aligned with the Paris Agreement. Specifically, the group is committed to directing financial flows to investments with a *warming potential* below the 1.5°C limit by 2050. Operating in an economy that is very fossil fuels intensive, AXA is working with experts[54] to develop measurement tools and methodologies to assess the *warming potential* of its assets, and make the necessary investment/divestment decisions.

In the food sector, Danone is also set to make a complete transition to a zero-carbon economy. The carbon neutrality by 2050 objective involves the entire value chain; Danone becomes responsible for the greenhouse gas emissions of the production cycle, from the farms to the billions of consumers in the world. How can it achieve this? On the one hand by reducing emissions, on the other hand by transforming agricultural practices, by eliminating deforestation from their supply chain, and finally by compensating for the remaining emissions.

Examples of companies that are taking this step abound, and they are a source of hope. They are not only multinationals or mega-organizations. Many SMEs are also run by leaders, perhaps you, who are contributing to this collective effort.

---

54 For example, AXA is a member of the in 2019 founded UN-convened Net-Zero Asset Owner Alliance - assembling 37 major institutional investors joining forces to accelerate the decarbonization of their portfolios (together more than $5.7 trillion) by 2050 and to measure and report on progress every five years.

Your climate actions can inspire your team. By choosing to bike to the office instead of driving, by deciding to print only on recycled paper (or not at all), or by switching off air conditioning, you are raising awareness among your employees. When these actions are fully integrated into your strategy, you multiply the impact of your efforts.

> *"Small streams make big rivers"*
>
> **Ovid**

In England, 75% of the population believes that business bears responsibility for protecting the environment[55]. In the Fall of 2021, a small earthquake could strike the UK! The country could become the first in the world to ratify a law requiring all companies to operate in a way that benefits not only shareholders but all stakeholders, including the climate! This bill *(The Better Business Act)* paves the way for a new paradigm: every commercial company, large or small, would be responsible for its social and environmental impact. Decisions taken must integrate this multifactorial perspective, rather than only considering the interests of shareholders – as is still far too often the case. According to this law, each company will have to share in an official report indicators related to its impact on people, on the planet and on profit. Supported by more than 500 companies (such as The Body Shop, Waitrose, Innocent or Patagonia), this bill was initiated by B Lab UK, an association bringing together the growing community of companies that have obtained B Corp certification in England.

Since 2006, the B Corp movement has brought together companies that want to turn business into a real force for the

55 Research by BBA - https://betterbusinessact.org/

common good, pursuing the goal of the three Ps - integrating people, planet and profit. Validated by a rigorous questionnaire (the BIA: Benefit Impact Assessment), B Corp certification is awarded to companies that integrate social, societal, and environmental objectives into their business model and decision-making. B Corps aim to be the best for the world rather than the best in the world. It's hard not to praise that intention.

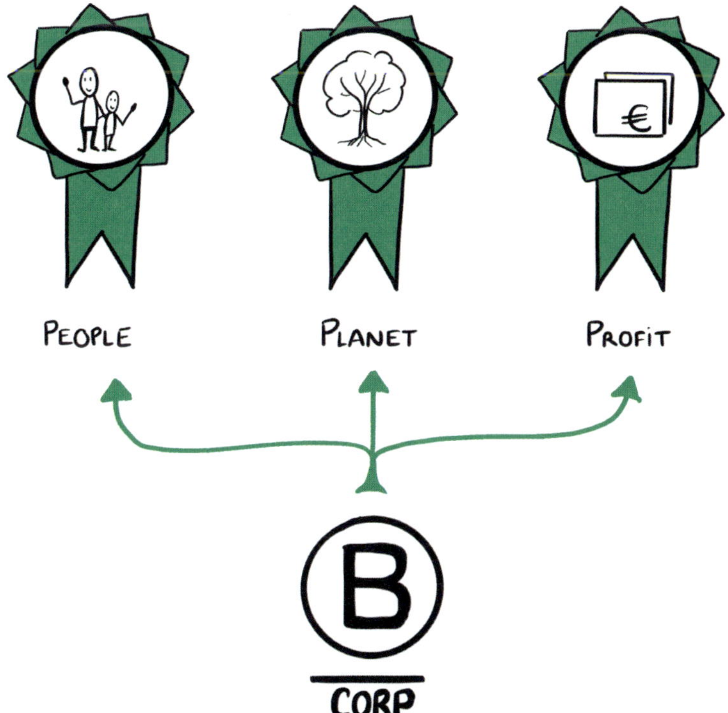

Rose Marcario, former CEO of outerwear brand Patagonia, was one of the pioneers in associating with this movement. Upon joining the company in 2008, she evaluated Patagonia's production processes and took drastic steps to reduce its negative impact on the environment, such as eliminating waste and reducing packaging materials. She believes that the B Corp movement is essential because business is not only about shareholders, but also about responsibility to the community and to the planet. The values and aspirations of the B Corp community are embodied in a *Declaration of Interdependence* signed by certified companies who, recognizing the interconnection that binds us, commit to act responsibly toward all stakeholders and future generations. To become a B Corp, companies must amend their bylaws to require the board of directors to strike a balance between profit and mission. This legal structure is called the *Benefit Corporation* in the United States, the *Società Benefit* in Italy, and in France it has inspired the *Société à mission*.

Courageous leaders, determined to move from intention to action, have embarked their teams on this process. Nearly 4000 companies in 74 countries have been certified to date. Many of these companies are SMEs, with some multinationals actively engaged in the process. Danone has proceeded with B Corp certification for several of its entities. Ben & Jerry, a subsidiary of Unilever, is also a B Corp.

With its 2500 employees worldwide, Swiss bank Lombard Odier has been a B Corp since 2019, determined to combine financial objectives with a societal mission. More than a declaration, it represents a commitment to respect sustainability criteria in their investments, and transparency in the monitoring of impact indicators. The bank promotes a circular, efficient, inclusive and clean economy.

Is this strategy a communication stunt or *green washing*? If you feel that way, think again. The B Corp certification, which is valid for 36 months, is only awarded after a thorough examination by independent bodies, ensuring that the necessary rating is obtained on the basis of a very demanding questionnaire of about 200 questions – the Benefit Impact Assessment mentioned above.

Can ecology be combined with profit?

Economy and ecology are often perceived as two opposing concepts. Yet they share the prefix *eco* (from the Greek, *oikos*), which refers to the management of the home. Reconciling economy and ecology is a necessity in order to unite the whole of society around current social and environmental issues.

Bertrand Piccard, one of the first to consider ecology through a profitability lens, is convinced that solving the climate crisis is possible by diffusing innovative and efficient technologies that will convince governments and companies to act. In the realm of his Solar Impulse Foundation, a panel of independent experts has evaluated over *1000 clean and profitable solutions*. From software that tracks your carbon footprint to a used plastic repair system, from vertical farms to a reusable diaper washing machine, these innovations from around the world cover all sectors. Assembled in a *Guide*[56], available online since April 2021, these verified solutions can be deployed on a large scale. In a pragmatic and practical way, this initiative aims to provide political and economic leaders with tools to achieve carbon neutrality goals.

The concrete examples and disruptive trends above generate collective awareness. This is the necessary step to accelerate

56 Solar Impulse Foundation – website and solutions: https://solarimpulse.com/efficient-solutions

the transition to a new economic model, integrating social and environmental impacts. The challenge for all of us is to take part in this transformation.

Leader-actor

As human beings, we have the extraordinary capacity to make conscious choices. I often insist on this notion of conscious choice which underscores our freedom. As a consequence of the development of our consciousness, we are responsible for our actions. In its original sense, responsibility emphasizes our capacity to respond (response-ability).

Whatever your sector and company size – small store, SME or multinational – you have a role to play in the fight against global warming. The fate of future generations depends on it, as does the survival of your company in a zero-carbon economy.

The magnitude of the threat requires leaders to acknowledge their share of responsibility for the situation we face today. Leadership is thus facing a major challenge: to accelerate the transformation of companies to create an economic model in which the environment is a stakeholder. The time when the leader's responsibility is limited to maximizing profits is over. The choice is yours: to suffer or to act?

Environmental initiatives, *eco-actions*, are flourishing in companies. Encouraging carpooling, consuming locally, eliminating plastic cups at the coffee machine, favoring less polluting industrial processes, are all useful. Beyond these everyday actions, today's leaders are called upon to become activists, influencers and inspirers.

As illustrated above by the *Better Business Act* in England, business leaders can lobby for more stringent legislation on social and environmental protection.

Companies have the power to influence government through their trade associations or chambers of commerce. By controlling the supply chain, it is up to you to require suppliers to assess their climate impact and to work with those who engage in the process. Finally, to reinforce your impact, communicating your environmental efforts is a way to inspire other leaders to take these steps.

> *"Courage is the first of the virtues because it makes all the others possible"*
>
> **Aristotle**

Being a change leader requires courage and determination. It is not the easiest path as it incorporates a multifactorial reality, but it is the resilient path - one that elevates and contributes to the common good.

To nurture your commitment, sharing with others who share your beliefs, is extremely helpful. Some professional associations bring together leaders who are convinced of the urgency of transforming our economic model to a more sustainable and planet-friendly one. The Regenerative Alliance[57], launched in 2020, supports leaders in the private and public sectors – across all industries – in this transition to a regenerative economy. By creating a space for peer-to-peer, expert-driven exchange, this community builds on the collective intelligence and collaboration of its members.

57 Regenerative Alliance - www.regenerative-alliance.org

The transformation of the economic world is underway, accelerated by leaders who are increasingly concerned by the world's future. In light of the current knowledge, it is up to you to consider your relationship with the environment as a dynamic opportunity for mutual enrichment. By expanding your professional responsibilities to include a social and environmental perspective, you give your leadership role a whole new scope. And suddenly, the question of the meaning of your professional activity touches your heart as a leader!

Bring your attention to the present moment and ask yourself these questions:

- When I make decisions in my daily work life, do I think about their impact on the environment?
- What could I do to be a more committed leader-actor?
- What eco-actions have I put in place in my team?
- Do we have a CSR policy?
- Do we integrate environmental impact criteria in the choice of our suppliers?
- Do I communicate regularly with my teams and the outside world about our climate commitments?

Ready to take action? Go to page 154 to make your choice in the *Practical Menu*.

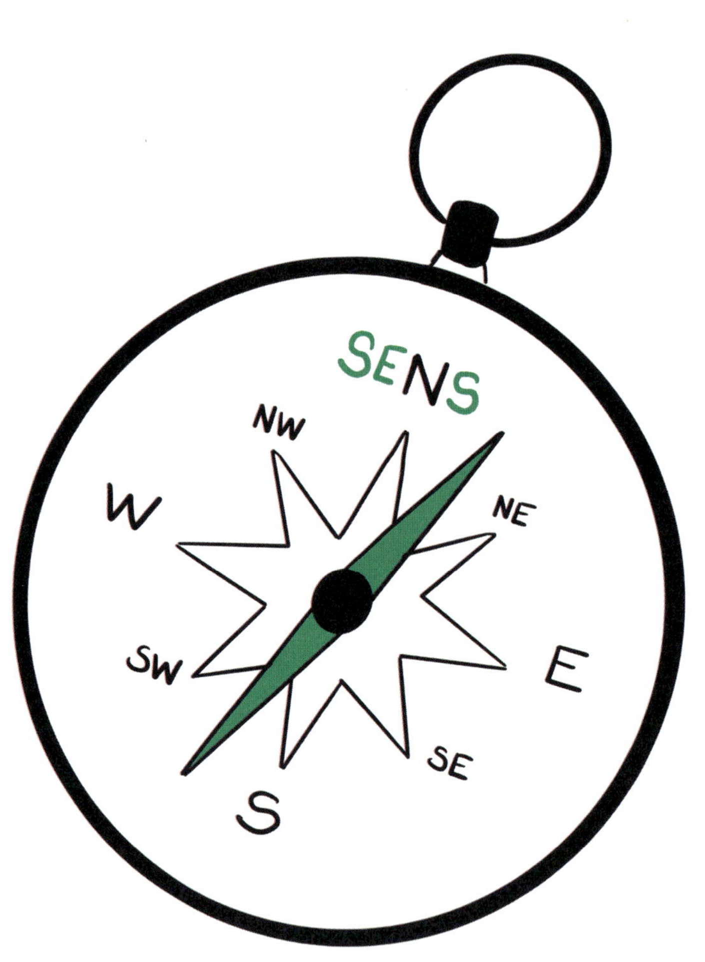
SENS
NW
W
NE
SW
E
SE
S

CHAPTER 5

THE QUESTION OF MEANING

"He who has a why to live can bear almost any how"

Friedrich Nietzsche

The quest for meaning has occupied mankind since the dawn of time. It is an important human need on both an individual and collective level. Endowed with a substantial reasoning ability, human beings seek to understand themselves, others, and the universe. This faculty in turn drives introspection and the search for keys that give meaning to one's existence.

In this chapter, we shall build upon the personal process and then move on to the collective one that I encourage you to initiate in your team. Right at the top of the resilience spiral, as illustrated in the introduction, the *spirit in action* sign reminds us of the importance of values, ethics and meaning - both individually and collectively.

Connecting to the question of meaning opens a level of sensitive awareness that illuminates life with new understanding and gives it another dimension. Being a resilient leader also means creating a work environment that fosters the realization of your company's purpose. It is important to identify this purpose and to ensure that everyone adheres to this cause that gives meaning to work well beyond, the undoubtedly necessary, financial results.

A personal approach

Who am I? What to do with my life? What is the meaning of my existence?

Finding answers to these deep and intimate questions is often the search of a lifetime, and not the focus of this book. Instead, let us try to enrich the questioning here. As in mathematics, understanding a question is the first necessary step to begin answering it.

The Merriam-Webster dictionary's definitions of *meaning*: the idea or thing that one intends to convey or is represented by a word, phrase or language – the idea that a person wants to express by using words or signs – the idea that is expressed in a work of writing or art.

Philosophers understand meaning as "the destination of human beings and their history, the reason for their existence and actions, the principle that gives human life its value[58]." The psychoanalytic perspective[59] emphasizes the need to integrate lived experiences and find direction in one's life, in order to nourish the quest for meaning. It is a question of establishing links between various aspects of a subjective experience (happy or unhappy), and to inscribe these elements in one's personal history, by situating them in space

58 N. BARAQUIN, *Dictionnaire de philosophie*, Armand Colin (2011).

59 F. LE HENAND, "La quête de sens", *Cahiers jungiens de psychanalyse*, vol. 125, n°1, pp19-30 (2008).

and time (the past, the present and the future that is opening up). This reflection is what gives these experiences meaning. A painful ordeal - e.g., a divorce, an illness, or the loss of one's job - can thus also be the source of certain positive developments: a rapprochement with one's family, the implementation of a new lifestyle, or the courage to launch a new professional project. And this development can give meaning to a negative experience.

For the psychiatrist and concentration camp survivor Viktor Frankl[60] (1905-1997), the most powerful antidote to the ills of our world is precisely *meaning*. What an extraordinary pioneer! Logotherapy, a therapeutic approach he created and disseminated in 1945, differs from psychoanalysis by focusing on the patient's future rather than his past. Logotherapy looks both at a person's reason for living (*logos* in Greek means "reason"), and at his efforts to discover one. Frankl contends that these efforts are a fundamental motivating force. He observed that, in the camps, the surviving prisoners were generally those who managed to visualize themselves into the future, with the aim of realizing an important personal project, or reuniting with their loved ones. Those who gave up, who had no more goals, let themselves die.

The quest for meaning, a healthy tension

The search for meaning can of course create a certain amount of tension, but a tension that is essential to mental health, according to Frankl. The awareness of this degree of tension between what we have already achieved and what we have

60 V. FRANKL, *Man's search for meaning*, Beacon Press (1959).

yet to achieve, between who we are and who we would like to become, gives meaning.

What human beings need is not a life without tension but to strive towards a goal, to accomplish a mission, to feel the call to achieve something.

Mental health is supposedly not based on an inner balance devoid of any tension, but on the meaning attributed to a situation, and a healthy dynamic process that aims at the realization of what we hold dear. Meaning is therefore both the goal and the direction, the path.

A malaise, or some sort of existential void, may arise if a human being is unsuccessful in finding a reason to live. Logotherapy speaks of *existential frustration*, that can lead to so-called *noogenic* neuroses; these neuroses do not originate in the psychological realm of the human being, but rather in his noogenic dimension (*noos* in Greek means "spirit"). In our time, the loss of meaning is unfortunately a widespread evil, and its manifestations are depression, addictions, or aggressiveness. The search for meaning can be substituted with the search for power which, when pushed to a certain point, may become addictive (earning more and more money), or with the search for immediate pleasures (compulsive shopping). Compensations that do not allow to move forward towards the discovery of the meaning of one´s life.

We do not suggest that life has one general meaning, shared by all. This is obviously very personal. Inspired by Viktor Frankl, I am convinced that we can attribute a meaning to each situation in life, at any given moment. We can attribute a meaning to a specific choice. Let us take Vincent, a young father who chooses to take three months off after the birth of his first baby, with the intention to share this special moment with his partner. Or the meaning one gives to a period of one´s life; for example, the realization of a professional ambition that leads Claudia to travel a lot, and to accept the sacrifices that this choice entails. Or the meaning of a project. I am thinking of a six-month trip we took with my husband and our four children in 2014, putting our professional careers on hold (and probably also at risk), with the objective of awakening our children´s curiosity and creating strong bonds between us.

Logotherapy teaches three main avenues to reveal the meaning of life, to discover a reason for being. The first is to achieve a work or a good deed. The second is to love something (the beauty of nature, a sport, an art) or someone. The third one, more difficult to apprehend, suggests giving a meaning to an inevitable suffering.

How to find the strength to live during the most inhuman trials?

Some people go through dramatic experiences. The loss of a child, torture, war, loneliness, an incurable disease, separation, bankruptcy, the list is endless. In the face of tragedy, one ultimate freedom remains: the attitude we adopt in these situations fate forces us to experience. It is a matter of transcending the ordeal. The notion of responsibility is reflected in our ability to respond – to make sense - of everything that happens to us, even in the most difficult circumstances.

Frankl invites us to cultivate *tragic optimism*. To acknowledge that meaning can be found in the midst of chaos, that hope can emerge from tragedy, that something positive can emerge from suffering, without removing the misery. This constitutes a resilient mindset, determined to grow through hardship, to learn from any situation, without denial or naivety.

We certainly have inspiring examples of people who have managed to make sense of tragedies. I think of my friend, Laurence Pian, who created the *Jan & Oscar Foundation* to support projects aimed at providing schooling for disadvantaged children in Thailand, following the deaths of Jan and Oscar – two of her four children – in the 2004 tsunami. Laurence's response to this tragedy, the creation of the Foundation, is a magnificent illustration of the ability to transcend inevitable suffering and find a path to hope, despite the gaping wound in her mother's heart.

Meaning and purpose are like beacons that provide light even in the darkest of times. They generate the positive emotions that keep you going and give you the courage to face adversity. Research has shown that those who have a conscious *reason to live* tend to live longer, healthier, and more mentally fit lives[61].

At the Resilience Institute, our research has demonstrated that having a purpose, a reason for being, is one of the key resilience factors for people. When this purpose serves a cause that goes beyond the individual person, creates value beyond the self and for society at large, then its power is multiplied.

Stone breaker or cathedral builder?

Why getting up every morning to go to work? Let us face it: for most people, working translates into *earning a living* to pay bills, have a roof over one´s head, fill the fridge, have some fun, etc. These are the primary motivations to go to work every morning, even if sometimes we do not feel like it. The second motivation is social. Work provides status and relationships. We here touch upon the limit of working from home, which considerably limits contacts, and so diminishes the power of this motivational lever. The third motivation is related to intrinsic pleasure – accomplishing interesting and meaningful activities. This reason drives people toward volunteer work, where the financial aspect is secondary.

We are generally, and conceivably, conditioned to consider our work life from the financial angle: money is after all a crucial factor that fulfills our need for security, as explained in Maslow´s pyramid. On the other hand, thinking of money as an end in itself, rather than as a means to achieve one´s aspirations, may lead to great disillusionment, a form of distortion of reality.

---

61 ASSOCIATION FOR PSYCHOLOGICAL SCIENCE, "Having a sense of purpose may add years to your life.", Science Daily (2014).

Given the amount of time we spend working, it comes as no surprise that we are also searching for meaning in our work. Meaning is based on the experience, perception, and interpretation of our reality. For work to be meaningful, it must provide satisfaction, match your interests or aspirations, use your skills, or stimulate your potential.

Let us take Julian, passionate about art, who has accepted a job as a salesclerk, an activity more in line with his parents' expectations than with his own aspirations. Julian really dislikes his job, even though he spends five days a week at it. His workdays are unsatisfying, and he disapproves the practices his boss put in place. Gradually, his spirits get lower. On the day Julien becomes aware of his deep aspirations and the set of values that guides him, he switches jobs and joins the communication team of a cultural center; Julien's life changes radically because his work, now more in line with his personal aspirations, has meaning in his eyes.

Why do you get up every morning to go to work?

Answering this question requires a thought process that involves defining a purpose or reason that gives meaning to what you do. In Japan, *ikigai* is a concept that refers to purpose.

Literally, *iki* means "life" and *gai* means "worthwhile". *Ikigai* is therefore a life worth living, where you are aligned with yourself. In the professional world, this philosophy purports that meaningful work strikes a balance between four components:

When you hold managerial responsibility, it is not just about your job, it is about the job of an entire team. In his book *Start with why*[62], Simon Sinek demonstrates how great leaders inspire their teams. The ability to clearly articulate *why* a company/team/activity exists, enables a leader to create powerful motivation and high commitment within his team.

62 S. SINEK, *Start with why*, Performance ED (2015).

Let us dive into the fable of the stone breaker, attributed to the French poet Charles Péguy (1873-1914), so as to illustrate how the meaning of work can be considered differently by different people.

On his way to Chartres, Charles Péguy sees a man on the side of the road breaking stones with a mallet. The man's gestures are marked by rage, his face is dark. Intrigued, Péguy stops and asks:

"What are you doing, sir?"

– You see," the man replied, "I'm breaking stones".

Unhappy, the poor man adds in a bitter tone: "My back hurts, I am thirsty, I am hungry". A little further along the path, our traveler sees another man who is also breaking rocks. But his attitude seems a little different. His face is more serene, and his gestures more harmonious.

"What do you do, sir?", Péguy asks again.

– I am a stone breaker. It's a hard job, you know, but it allows me to feed my wife and children".

Catching his breath, he sketches a slight smile and adds: "And then, come on, I'm in the open air, there are probably worse situations than mine".

Further on, our man meets a third stone breaker. His attitude is totally different. He shows a frank smile, and he brings down his mace, with enthusiasm, on the pile of stones. Such ardor is beautiful to see! What are you doing?

" asks Péguy.

– Me," replies the man, "I'm building a cathedral!"

How would your employees answer the following two questions: What do you do for a living? Why do you work in this team?

Anyone can easily answer the first question; fewer are able to clearly articulate *why* they are doing this particular work.

May some clarification on the purpose of your company or team be a powerful lever to create a sense of belonging, to support performance and to strengthen collective resilience? Possibly also a way to attract and retain the best talents? What if the identification of a *raison d'être*, was a way to contribute to society, to create societal value, beyond the financial goals? Could it all give a whole new meaning to your role as a leader?

The greatest leaders have demonstrated time and again that in order to bring about change in oneself, in a community or in society, it is necessary to give meaning to this change, to identify the relevance that can move mountains. The raison d'être is the spark that sustains the vision, the confidence, the determination, and the energy to continue.

If the meaning of your work gives an answer to the question *why*, then your *values* answer the question *how*. How do you reach that goal? Like a compass, values indicate the most coherent direction. Collectively, values express the way we work together. When, in a team, we can evaluate decisions from a well-understood values matrix, important choices are much easier to make, and outcomes more fulfilling. Beware the trap of nice, but meaningless, words posted on the walls of a reception. The real issue is translating these values into actions or expected behaviors, well beyond the theory. Who is in a better position than your employees to transform concepts into concrete actions that concern them directly? Take some time collectively, think it over, and let yourself be surprised by the common creativity in identifying these *values-actions*, specific to your team.

Below are some examples of values-actions. Please note their subjectivity, and relevance only if they are the result of collective reflection.

- Diversity → *We welcome and value diverse opinions in the team.*
- Innovation → *We encourage innovative ideas and out-of-the-box thinking*
- Benevolence → *We respect everyone and take care of the relationships inside and outside the team.*
- Responsibility → *We take responsibility for our actions*
- Safety → *We follow safety procedures for the benefit of all.*

Bring your attention to the present moment to ask yourself these few questions:

- What motivates me to go to work each morning?
- Have I found my *ikigai* ?
- What is the purpose of my company (or my team)?
- Am I able to answer this question clearly and inspiringly?
- How often do I remind people of our common purpose in team meetings?
- What are the values-actions that guide our behaviors within the team?

The *raison d'être* for the benefit of all

In 2015, all member states of the United Nations officially adopted the 17 *Sustainable Development Goals* (or SDGs) to be achieved by 2030, in order to respond to the relentless evidence that the world needs a more sustainable approach. This resolution, adopted on October 21, 2015, and articulated in a 38-page document[63], details an ambitious program that aims to transform the world - no more, no less.

This action plan challenges the global economic model relying on the creation of ever more material wealth and aspires to implement more sustainable development for all – economic, social, and environmental. Seventeen goals provide a roadmap for addressing the challenges of poverty, inequality, climate, environmental degradation, prosperity, peace, and justice.

The SDGs are a reminder of the interconnections between all the aspects of the problem and the urgency of bringing all parties together to accelerate a necessary societal transformation. Businesses are called upon to *do their part* and contribute to the emergence of a sustainable future for all.

Some leaders heard the call and, starting in 2015, have been rethinking their *raison d'être*, to make it converge with the SDGs.

In August 2018, the *Business Roundtable* - a group of leaders from the 200 largest U.S. companies (totaling more than 20 million employees) – made a noteworthy and remarkable

63 Resolution adopted by the United Nations General Assembly on September 25, 2015, "Transforming Our World: 2030 Agenda for Sustainable Development": https://undocs.org/fr/A/RES/70/1

1. NO POVERTY
2. ZERO HUNGER
3. GOOD HEALTH AND WELL BEING
4. QUALITY EDUCATION
5. GENDER EQUALITY
6. CLEAN WATER AND SANITATION
7. AFFORDABLE AND CLEAN ENERGY
8. DECENT WORK AND ECONOMIC GROWTH
9. INDUSTRY, INNOVATION AND INFRASTRUCTURE
10. REDUCED INEQUALITIES
11. SUSTAINABLE CITIES AND COMMUNITIES
12. RESPONSIBLE CONSUMPTION AND PRODUCTION
13. CLIMATE ACTION
14. LIFE BELOW WATER
15. LIFE ON LAND
16. PEACE, JUSTICE AND STRONG INSTITUTIONS
17. PARTNERSHIPS FOR GOALS

announcement[64]: that an organization's purpose must serve the interests of all stakeholders – customers, employees, suppliers, communities, and shareholders – and create shared value. This announcement is a major departure from traditional shareholder-based governance principles. It represents a leap forward for the concept of corporate social responsibility (CSR) and states the essential role of organizations in a society when their leaders are guided by a concern for the aspirations of all stakeholders. Signatories not only commit to serve shareholders, but to create value for their customers, invest in employee training, treat suppliers ethically and respectfully, and support the communities they operate in.

Is raison d'être a buzzword, a passing concept, a luxury concern? Or is it a crucial strategic issue? A growing body of research suggests that clarifying the purpose of a company – large or small – has multiple benefits, including performance.

When purpose is at the core, it influences decisions at all levels. A study by Deloitte[65] found that companies that stayed true to their purpose during the Covid-19 pandemic strengthened the bond of trust with their customers; 79% of respondents (from a large global sample of more than 2,500 people) remembered brands that supported their customers, employees, or communities during the crisis. There are many ways to show support: the bank that extends payment schedules, the hotel that offers overnight stays to hospital staff who have been on the front lines for so many months, or the concert hall that turns into a vaccination center. When the response to a

---

64 Business Roundtable Commitment: https://opportunity.businessroundtable.org/ourcommitment/

65 S. KOUNKEL, A. SILVERSTEIN, K. PEETERS, "Purpose: Built to flourish", Deloitte Global Marketing Trends Report (2021).

crisis is aligned with a purpose that connects the company to its role in society, it's a win-win! The same study shows that when societal purpose guides organizations, they become 30% more innovative than others. In addition to attracting the best people, these organizations have a 40% higher talent retention rate than their competitors.

It is noteworthy that young professionals are increasingly sensitive to these issues. Each generation is naturally conditioned by the circumstance in which it evolves. The *baby boomer* generation (born between 1940 and 1959), marked by the post-war period, was particularly keen to ensure a certain material comfort. The X Generation (1960 - 1979) tends to assert its status through its consumer choices, while the millennials – also known as Generation Y[66](born between the early 80s and the late 90s) – are looking for experiences and meaning. One research found that 75% of them are willing to earn less for a job that serves a societal cause. They read corporate missions and value statements to guide their job search. This trend is even stronger among Generation Z (born after 1995), whose members are entering the workforce and want to work for socially responsible employers.

Demonstrating that your professional activity has meaning and *does good* for something other than your wallet is now essential to motivate these young people, who by 2025 will represent 75% of the workforce!

Should we sacrifice performance for meaning? Absolutely not!

Companies that decide, through their activities, to be at the service of all stakeholders are more profitable in the long

---

66 A. PETERS, "Most millennials would take a pay cut to work at an environmentally responsible company," Fast Company (2019).

term than those whose model, most often based on the short term, serves only shareholders[67].

Organizations guided by a societal purpose achieve better performance, attract and retain talent, while increasing employee engagement and customer satisfaction. Everyone benefits.

Clarifying your company's purpose is the first step; if the initiative remains at the slogan stage, the impact on your team will be limited, or nil. Only concrete actions that materialize the effort can prove the coherence and authenticity of the approach. Purpose then becomes a powerful instrument, a compass helping in strategic choices and guiding managerial decisions. It is not about changing the world, but about boosting the positive impact of the work of your entire team. What is true for large organizations is also true for small entities: meaning serves performance, while generating the multiple benefits described above.

Like any existential question, taking time to reflect is crucial to answer it correctly. What is the impact of your activities on society at large, but also more directly on your customers, suppliers, the community in which you operate? Is your company's purpose a univocal declaration by the management? What is the value of a team's *raison d'être* if its own members do not believe in it? A collective answer to the question "why does our team exist?" is a powerful revelator of energy and creativity. Involving your employees in this reflection is the best way to get their support for a common goal. Think about what is most essential at the heart of your activity, beyond your products or services.

The AXA insurance group unveiled its purpose in 2020: "Acting for human progress by protecting what matters."

---

67 D.J. FERRAN, K. SPERRY, "The Torrey Project" (2019).

Luminus, EDF's Belgian subsidiary active in the production and distribution of energy, clearly communicates its vision: "To build a CO2-neutral energy future, reconciling preservation of the planet, well-being, and development thanks to electricity and innovative solutions and services." Danone aims to "Bring health through food to as many people as possible." The chemical group Solvay's *raison d'être* is to "Bond people, elements and ideas to reinvent progress." In 2019, the French telecom operator Orange inscribed its purpose in its articles of association: "To be a trusted player that gives everyone the keys to a responsible digital world." This vision did not come from nowhere; it was co-constructed in 2019 by involving the employees of the entire organization.

By giving itself a purpose, a company becomes part of a societal project and defines its role – beyond its mere economic activity. In a situation where capitalism is reaching its limits and must converge towards societal interest, the raison d'être becomes a central issue, not only for large organizations or multinational corporations, but also for smaller structures. A carpenter can commit to contribute to the well-being of customers while promoting local and traditional craftsmanship. A hairdresser can engage in creating a moment of relaxation and give back confidence to her clients. The meaning of the commitment of a school director can be to stimulate curiosity and prepare future generations to be responsible actors.

What is the meaning of your work and the reason for your team's existence? The resilient leader is aware of the world's challenges and asks the question of meaning, whatever his scope of influence. Once established and formulated in an understandable way, you must diffuse this raison d'être within your ecosystem by making it explicit to all stakeholders. In this way, you manage to regularly remind everyone of the meaning of your activity, and how the team's decisions honor this purpose.

Since May 2019, in France, the Pacte law (mentioned in the previous chapter) gives companies the opportunity to include their societal mission in their articles of association. On top of their raison d'être, these *companies with a mission* also clarify their environmental and/or social objectives, while establishing a procedure to monitor progress. The pursuit of a social mission is not in contradiction with the pursuit of profit. It is a counterweight to prevailing short-termism guiding shareholder decisions and a solution for putting economic performance at the service of the common good. In 2020, the dairy giant Danone was the first exchange listed company to choose this model of corporation.

Providing your team with a purpose that broadens its scope, you support collective resilience. It is both an anchor that allows facing tougher times by *staying the course*, and an aspiration to play a positive societal role that elevates the entire team.

> *"The purpose of an organization is to enable ordinary human beings to do extraordinary things."*
>
> **Peter Drucker**

The leader's legacy

Since 2008, my work as a professional consultant and coach has tremendously inspired me, for many reasons. I have witnessed similar patterns in conversations with leaders from a variety of cultural, sectorial, contextual, and social backgrounds. By creating a space for constructive reflection, the notion of time expands, we revert to the past and what it teaches us; we look forward to the future and what lies ahead. The leader's legacy topic is a tipping point in the discussion. The lasting mark left by a leader is measured by what he leaves behind. A legacy is a transmissible *good*. Despite its importance, I am not talking about a *tangible* legacy - leaving a well-managed position, passing on a financially healthy business, generating profits, etc. – but rather the intangible or *spiritual* legacy as we describe it at the Resilience Institute. *Putting your spirit in action* is the 7th pillar of personal resilience (see Chapter 2); what falls under *ethics, values* and *meaning*.

You elevate the debate by thinking about what you will leave to your team or to the company and imagining your role beyond your immediate interest. A recognition of your influence, beyond your presence. The CEO of a multinational company evidently affects thousands of people by his decisions. You are not a CEO but *simply* responsible for a team or a small company? Do not underestimate the impact you have on your entire ecosystem, directly or indirectly: your colleagues, collaborators, customers, suppliers, but also the surrounding environment. Understanding your impact renders you more conscious, responsible, a more resilient leader. By caring about the common good and leaving a positive heritage, you take better care of relationships and make choices that are aligned with the purpose of your business.

The resilient leader is essentially inspiring by way of his personal consistency and his *guiding by example*. He creates a safe space within the team for constructive dialogue around the question of meaning. He involves his staff to clarify the team's *raison d'être* and the *meaning* of each person's role.

Think about that first stone breaker: had he seen his contribution to a larger project, to a major collective achievement in line with his aspirations, would he not have been more fulfilled and committed? The alignment between the *individual* meaning (the meaning of my role) and the *collective* meaning (the team's *reason for being*) triggers the resonance that is source of innovation and sustainable performance.

Ready to take action? Go to page 155 to make your selection from the *Practical Menu*.

PRACTICAL MENU

"Choose always the way that seems the best, however rough it may be; custom will soon render it easy and agreeable."

Pythagoras

In this last chapter, I address a subject that is dear to me: taking action. If you have read this book, it is because you are sensitive to current developments and feel that changes are taking place. More and more organizations understand that new skills are needed, but are either unable to cultivate them or are still terribly conditioned by the old paradigm that is no longer up to the challenges of today's world. Many leaders know something needs to change, but do not know where to start.

In your managerial role, you are aware that your choices, your attitude, your behavior, your decisions have an impact that goes beyond yourself. it is about inspiring and leading by example. Resilience skills can be learned, trained, and cultivated. But embracing a concept or an idea is not enough. Action is crucial for the advancement of your *Resilience*

Quotient; action precedes change and brings results. Just as being aware of the benefits of exercise, but doing none, will not strengthen your muscles, so too with resilience, awareness is necessary but not sufficient. There can be no results without action. Without action, dreams and ambitions remain dreams and ambitions.

From intention to action

Are you sometimes overwhelmed by the magnitude of the task? Are you frustrated by the slow pace of change in the face of the urgency of the transformations needed in your company and in the world? Do you tend to feel guilty or dramatize the current situation? Anxiety-provoking, sad or depressing information can certainly provoke withdrawal, anger, denial or fear. This is the time to roll up your sleeves and choose resilience.

By definition, a leader's zone of influence is more or less large. This zone of influence starts with oneself (self-leadership), which makes each of us a leader, even without a team to guide.

In his best-selling book, Stephen R. Covey (1932-2012) makes the distinction between proactive people, who focus on what they can do, change or influence, and reactive people, who focus on what they cannot control. He thus defines the circle of concerns as the set of events or elements under our control, and those over which we feel we have no influence. Depending on the person, the list is of variable length: the weather, the state of the economy, what your colleagues are doing (or not doing!), global warming, political decisions, etc. The circle of influence includes everything you feel you have influence over. Of course, the scope of this second circle also varies depending on your position: the President of the United States or the CEO of Google have a wider circle of influence than you and me.

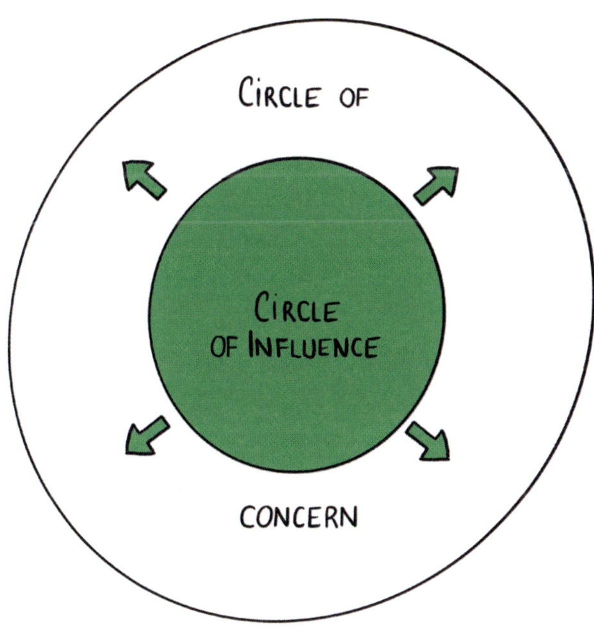

By focusing your time and energy on your circle of influence, you can make effective changes. As a result, that circle - and therefore your influence – will tend to grow. Conversely, by directing your energy towards the circle of concerns beyond your control, you give them too much attention and reduce your power of influence, since your energy is elsewhere. Understanding your circle of influence is a crucial aspect of your leadership. Proactive people will see their circle of influence increase, while reactive people will see their circle of influence decrease. In some cases, inaction is the wisest choice: letting go of what I cannot control and freeing up energy and creativity to act where I can have an impact. The Stoic philosopher Epictetus (50-125 B.C.) already pointed to this exercise of discernment[68]: distinguishing what depends on us from what does not, in order to direct our action where it has the largest impact. For Epictetus, this perspective can transform our view of what happens to us by becoming aware of our freedom to respond to any event.

By avoiding victimization and choosing responsibility (responsiveness), you become the architect of your future. By encouraging your team to adopt this proactive attitude, you create a bridge between a vision and its realization. Action is not an end in itself, it is the means to progress. As suggested throughout the chapters, consciously cultivating a relationship with yourself, others, the environment, and with the question of meaning, is the path to resilience. Through your actions and decisions, you will strengthen your *Resilience Quotient*.

The importance of habits

Did you know that over 40% of our actions are automatic[69]? They are carried out without your knowledge, for better or for worse. In your professional context too, habits shape the leader you are.

Habits are behaviors that you adopt automatically because you repeat them frequently. This repetition creates a mental association between a situation (stimulus) and an action

---

68 F. BERNARD, *Manager avec les philosophes*, Dunod (2016).

69 C. DUHIGG, *The power of habits*, Penguin Random House (2012).

(behavior), so that when the stimulus occurs, one adopts the behavior automatically - that is, without even thinking about it. A new habit is therefore built around 3 components: a stimulus (the conditions that favor the establishment of a new habit), an action (the behavior triggered by the stimulus), and finally the reward (the consequence of the new habit). This reward can be the feeling of vitality after a good night's sleep, the satisfaction of a constructive meeting or the feeling of accomplishment that comes with a successful project. The more this *stimulus-action-reward* loop is repeated, the more it takes root in your brain and finally becomes a habit.

The same pattern applies within a team: create the work environment that fosters the behaviors you want to spread, explicitly share the *why* of the habits you are trying to create, and make sure the *reward* is valuable to everyone.

Consider this Japanese company that understands the importance of micro-naps to sustain its workforce's energy and productivity throughout the day. Employees are *educated* to understand the benefits of this practice, which is culturally more accepted in Asia than in the West. In this organization, the light decreases between 13.00 and 13.30. This is the perfect stimulus to start a micro-nap. The condition is thus created to establish a new habit. The expected reward is a higher level of attention in the afternoon, and therefore more constructive work.

Another example of the creation of a new collective habit: a team leader suggested to her team to put their phones or tablets in a basket at the entrance to the meeting room, convinced of the importance of *presence* and active listening. Everyone quickly realized how much more effective and enjoyable these *in-person* meetings were for everyone, despite some initial reluctance. Or the CEO who systematically starts each team meeting with a 3-minute reminder of the company's mission and values, before diving into the financial results. These practices are not trivial; your attitude and behavior largely influence the attitude and behavior that dominate your team. The leader's exemplarity is at the heart of an approach to increase a team's *Resilience Quotient*, just as the management team's exemplarity is crucial to inspiring an entire organization.

But how long does it take for a practice to become a habit?

Research on this topic varies. In the 1960s, Dr. Maxwell Maltz, a plastic surgeon, found that it took an average of 21 days for a patient to become accustomed to a new mental image or to the disappearance of an amputated limb. He wrote a best-seller, *Psycho-Cybernetics*, in which he mentioned that a habit takes 21 days to become established, albeit without any real scientific basis. Years later, a study[70] conducted at the University of London (UCL) concluded that it takes an average of 66 days for a new behavior to become automatic, and therefore a habit.

Why does stepping out of one's comfort zone often induce a feeling of apprehension in human beings? Resistance to change is often linked to the fear of the unknown. The human brain is allergic to uncertainty, a condition associated by reflex and by default with the possibility of danger. Our brain being more sensitive to the negative than to the positive, we tend to perceive the possible losses linked to change rather than what we have to gain. Hence the need to understand, communicate, and anticipate the benefits (the reward) of implementing new behaviors.

The Chinese proverb, attributed to Lao Tzu (571-531 BC), recalls this wisely: *a journey of a thousand miles begins with*

---

70 P. LALLY, "How are habits formed: modelling habit formation in the real world", European Journal of Social Psychology, vol 40, pp 998-1009 (2010).

a first step. You have to go gradually, step by step, to reach your goals. Consistency and regularity are essential for a lasting change. That is why creating new habits is so helpful. At the Resilience Institute, we put a lot of emphasis on daily routines and habits. This is true on a personal level. It is also true on a professional level. I have observed and experienced how following five golden rules increases the chances of successfully instilling new practices.

1. **One at a time:** choose a new practice, commit to making it a new habit, and resist the temptation to change too many behaviors at once. This is what the small steps method - or Japanese Kaizen method (*kai* means "change", *zen* means "good") - teaches, encouraging small, concrete, simple, daily improvements.

2. **Explain:** be clear about why you are forming a new habit. If it involves your team, clarify what motivates taking up a new habit. This seems obvious, yet it is an often-overlooked step.

3. **Stimulus:** set up a trigger/environment or situation that will encourage the new behavior.

4. **Regularity:** repeat the behavior with discipline and confidence until it becomes automatic.

5. **Reward:** Be aware of the beneficial consequences of a new habit or behavior; share them explicitly with your team.

REWARD
REGULARITY
STIMULUS
EXPLAIN
ONE AT A TIME

Concrete actions to reinforce your RQ

You now know that habits are the key to increase competence. Whether it is in business, health, sports, or a passion. Make your choice in the following menu built around the themes discussed in the different chapters. It goes without saying that this is not an exhaustive list but a range of practices that can complement what you are already doing.

RELATION WITH ONESELF

Create calm and regenerate yourself

- Practice a breathing exercise at least once a day (count to 4 when inhaling and 6 to 1 when exhaling - 3 times in a row)
- Do a spinal twist several times a day
- Take regular micro-breaks during the workday
- Visualize a quiet, inspiring place for 1 minute before an important meeting
- Listen to relaxing music
- Practice deep relaxation before going to sleep (e.g. a *body scan*)
- Schedule some *me time* in your calendar for the week
- Close your eyes and relax your face
- Reconnect with nature
- Put things in perspective by projecting yourself into the future

Cultivate physical vitality

- Stretch for 10 minutes every morning
- Walk 30 minutes a day, 5 times a week
- Stand up every 20 minutes
- Hold standing or walking meetings
- Adjust your posture (back straight, shoulders down, heart open) sitting or standing
- Eat mindfully / more slowly
- Provide healthy snacks for cravings during the day
- Take a 20-minute power nap, 3 times a week
- Avoid screens one hour before going to sleep
- Wake up at the same time every day - including weekends

Engage your emotions

- In the evening, write down the emotions felt during the day, and so enrich your emotional vocabulary
- Cultivate gratitude by thinking about what went well during the day (www)
- Recognize what you can be proud of
- Admire nature
- Anticipate an enjoyable experience
- Recall a pleasant memory
- Create a quick win
- Celebrate the achievement of a goal
- Enjoy a touch of lightness
- Respond rather than react / avoid knee-jerk reactions

Train your mind

- Clarify priorities for the week/day
- Identify an intention each morning on how you want to live the day
- Practice mono-tasking
- Remove distractions to help with focus
- Work *offline* for 30 minutes in the morning / 30 minutes in the evening
- Be more selective and aware of the information you consume / produce. Avoid infobesity!
- Learn something new
- Focus your energy on your zone of influence
- Say *NO* while being aware of what you say *YES* to
- Tidy up your workspace

Put your spirit in action

- Set aside 5 minutes of personal reflection each day
- Experience mindfulness over a cup of tea/coffee
- Practice a contemplative exercise (centering, inner calm, prayer, meditation or other), 10 minutes a day
- Take your nose out of the water / get some perspective and look at a situation from a broader perspective
- Appreciate the present moment
- Provoke joy (and enjoy it)
- Plan one activity per week that is an optimal experience
- Read an inspirational text
- Plan a retreat or a personal development workshop
- Maintain the quality of your relationships

RELATION WITH OTHERS

Impact and authenticity

- Take risks and dare to be real
- Respect and communicate your own limits and those of your colleagues
- Show your emotions in a fair and appropriate way
- Admit your mistakes and insist on what you learn from them
- Apologize when it is justified
- Ask for help when you feel the need

A team, a safe space

- Share information transparently
- Create a culture of feedback within the team
- Develop collectively by learning from each other's mistakes
- Give everyone a voice in team meetings
- Welcome and value different opinions

Attention control and focus

- Have an alert posture that favors your attention
- Understand the components of presence
- Decide to be fully present during team meetings
- Encourage everyone to keep their phones and tablets away from meetings
- Keep meetings short (45 or 50 minutes) to maintain everyone's attention

Create proximity at a distance

- Create forums for formal and informal discussions within the team
- Involve the team to define the optimal communication intervals
- Get to know your colleagues and your staff as people (and not just for their professional role)
- Identify affinities, what you have in common with others
- Be available for quality conversations with everyone

Empathy and compassion at work

- Practice active listening (listening with ears, eyes, heart, and full attention) and show engagement (nodding or inviting further input)
- Read non-verbal cues
- Acknowledge and understand the other´s perspective; summarize what you have heard to clarify agreements but also possible disagreements
- Care for others with kindness
- Act with courage and compassion with the real intention of understanding, helping, or relieving

The posture of the leader-coach

- Understand the different leadership styles and reinforce the one(s) you are less familiar with
- Listen more (therefore, speak less) with the intention of learning and understanding
- Ask open-ended questions to encourage expression
- Ask closed questions to encourage clarification

- Ask powerful questions to unleash creativity
- Generate enthusiasm and confidence

Generate positive emotions within the team

- Celebrate small victories or steps towards a collective goal
- Thank the team more often for their contributions
- Create the conditions for an optimal team experience
- Project the team towards a positive future

Communicate with realistic optimism

- Acknowledge the unknowns and areas of uncertainty with humility while maintaining a confident and assertive tone
- Have a grounded and open posture that exudes confidence (standing, back straight, shoulders down, heart open)
- Express optimism about meeting challenges as a team
- Value the skills around the table
- Remind everyone that challenges make you grow

RELATION WITH THE ENVIRONMENT

Appreciate the beauty of nature

- Take regular walks in nature
- Marvel at a beautiful landscape
- Feel the *overview effect* by observing the Earth with a wider mental perspective
- (Learn to) grow a vegetable garden
- Integrate green plants in your work environment

Inform yourself and inform others

- Read scientific reports from experts (such as the IPCC report) to develop your knowledge of environmental issues
- Develop your critical thinking skills by consulting various sources on the subject of global warming
- Participate in engaged conversations on the topic
- Address the issue within your team
- Read the *European Green Deal*

Be a responsible leader

- Measure and understand the carbon footprint of your team / company
- Guide your team towards carbon neutrality by taking concrete measures / choose the eco-actions to adopt with your team
- Integrate CSR (Corporate Social Responsibility) dimensions into decision making and business conduct in general
- Join an association (such as the Regenerative Alliance) that supports responsible leaders in the energy transition
- Communicate internally and externally about your team's / company's climate commitments

THE QUESTION OF MEANING

Personal approach

- Welcome and stimulate questioning
- Create time to reflect on what goes beyond the day-to-day operations and touches deeper dimensions
- Read inspiring books to support your quest

- Consider a *personal coaching* approach
- Learn from adversity in any situation
- Identify your personal *ikigai* (see page 126)
- Make choices that are consistent with your purpose
- Act with integrity and in line with your personal values
- Be aware of the impact you want to have today
- Project yourself 40 years from now and reflect on your legacy as a leader

Collective approach

- Create time with the team to reflect on the purpose and impact of your activity
- Communicate your purpose to all stakeholders
- Collectively identify the values you want to honor and translate them into values-actions
- Start each team meeting with a reminder of the purpose and the values-actions that guide you
- Integrate the values-actions into the employee evaluation grid
- Define and implement measures of success beyond financial criteria
- Integrate the SDGs (Sustainable Development Goals) into the evaluation of the societal contribution of our activity
- Put purpose at the heart of decision making
- Include purpose in your organization´s bylaws
- Consider B Corp certification for your organization
- Consider a formal group commitment with other companies

CONCLUSION

"No problem can be solved from the same level of consciousness that created it."

Albert Einstein

As painful as they are, crises can be awareness accelerators and the source of opportunities. The Chinese expression for crisis (Wei-ji) helps as a reminder. Composed of two characters (危机), one meaning *danger* and the other *opportunity*, it implies that there is always an opportunity in every crisis.

The Covid-19 pandemic has highlighted the interdependence between countries and between the political, economic, and social sectors. This global outbreak has also revealed the potential for mobilization and impact, an accelerator of transition, despite the suffering it has caused. From this perspective, it represents a historic opportunity that invites us to reconsider our priorities, our way of life and our approach to work. What is expected of leaders has been profoundly modified. Acknowledging the positive and negative externalities any company generates for all its stakeholders is becoming urgent. Organizations must rethink their role and mission within society. Acting in a complex system whose parts are interdependent, a company can become a lever of transformation to bring about a new, more just business model, based on the common good.

Confronted with a global situation characterized by uncertainty and the loss of bearings, leaders have a choice to make, either to believe that what has worked in the past will be the solution to today's challenges, or to seize the opportunity of a necessary transformation. The stakes are immense, but the roadmap is clear: to humanize the company, to mobilize teams by choosing the path of resilience, and together create a positive future for all stakeholders.

The impact of the resilient leader is proportional to the strength of the relationship he manages to create with himself, with others and with the environment at large.

In this book, I wanted to emphasize the magnitude of change those nurturing these connections with humanity and humility can inspire, while using *meaning* as an inner compass. Being a resilient leader is not a title but a state of mind, a state of being, a posture.

Above all, it is a path of personal transformation, guided by introspection, reflection, and practice. Resilient leaders understand that taking care of oneself is a necessary condition for taking care of others. In a continuous process, they sense that deep self-awareness allows for a greater impact. They mobilize all their inner resources to bounce back from difficulties and grow through trials. They put in place an effective routine to deal with the pressure of daily life and manage their energy. They are authentic and guided by positive intentions.

Being a resilient leader is also having the courage to develop a fully human leadership, valuing resilient skills in a team, and integrating them into training plans. Resilient leaders build trust and maintain a constructive management culture in all circumstances. They generate positive emotions and radiate a joy less dependent on external conditions than on their inner strength.

Finally, it means including all stakeholders in the equation and taking part in the construction of a more inclusive, more responsible, and more regenerative economic world.

Alone, we can do little or nothing.

Too many people wait for others to act first or for regulations to impose the necessary changes. The strength of the leader is the audacity to undertake and to unite around an inspiring vision while generating hope, courage, confidence, and enthusiasm.

By cultivating our *Resilience Quotient* (and that of our teams), in our respective zones of influence, we collectively become conscious actors in the process of creating a positive future.

POSTWORD
by Thomas Buberl CEO of AXA Group

The Covid-19 pandemic and the ensuing upheavals have tested our individual and collective resilience as rarely in recent history. This sudden and brutal materialization of health risks is in effect symptomatic of a new age of uncertainty we must become accustomed to. In this era of increasingly recurrent, rapid, and profound transformations, adapting and bouncing back are therefore indispensable qualities. Being resilient has become a necessity for all of us, both personally and professionally.

While we can only agree on its benefits, resilience remains too often mysterious or inaccessible. A concept that is as necessary for coping with hardship as it is desirable because of its promise of improvement, resilience is nurtured more than it is decreed, practiced more than it is formalized. With talent, Alexia Michiels delivers the keys to understanding it, and meticulously reveals the secrets of a more resilient life.

By exploring the dimensions of our relationship with ourselves, with others and with nature that all strengthen our Resilience Quotient, Alexia Michiels invites us to become aware of our weaknesses in order to better tame them, while at the same time fostering our strengths in order to take greater advantage of them. She skillfully composes a detailed analysis of the dimensions that make up *resilience* and translates them into concrete precepts and recommendations.

For professionals, and particularly for managers and business leaders, including myself, reading this book provides a wealth of understanding, exercises and, one might say, recipes that can be applied in the short and long term to develop oneself and others. I have fully comprehended the importance of resilience during the difficult period we have been going through, during which my daily concern was to safeguard my teams, fully aware of the challenge that the recovery would represent.

On a personal level, I have no doubt that at the end of this book, everyone will have found the observations, advice and concepts that can be applied to their daily lives as a way to maintain and strengthen their resilience and to move towards greater meaning.

Finally, as an insurer, I would like to emphasize the relevance of this book, whose central theme is so closely related to my profession. Indeed, if insurance contributes to the material resilience of individuals and communities, the intimate approach to resilience discussed in this book is particularly complementary.

In sum, Alexia Michiels has authored a book that is both conceptually fruitful and highly valuable in practice.

JAN & OSCAR FOUNDATION

100% of this book's royalties are donated to the Jan & Oscar Foundation www.fondationjan-oscar.ch

On December 26, 2004, a tsunami in Asia causes the death of thousands of people, including two Swiss boys: Jan, aged 12, and Oscar, his little brother aged 8. This tragedy generates a wave of solidarity that led to the creation of the Jan & Oscar Foundation in June 2005.

Laurence Pian, mother of four children, including Jan and Oscar, is the founder and president of the Foundation. Giving meaning to the tragedy that affected her family, Laurence devotes her energy, courage and determination to projects aimed at educating underprivileged children in rural Thailand. Over the past 16 years, more than 50 projects have been completed, including constructions of schools, scholarships, environmental education programs, and drinking water installations in remote villages, all of which have made a difference in the lives of the children involved - children who have been marginalized by extreme poverty.

Laurence is a radiant woman and a tremendous example of resilience who greatly inspires me. I am also deeply convinced that education is the path to progress; for these children, as for our own, it is the only possible avenue to a better future.

> *"Education is the most powerful weapon which you can use to change the world."*

Nelson Mandela

ACKNOWLEDGEMENTS

Transitioning to resilient leadership is a transformative journey. When I began drafting this book, I had no idea how much my research would advance my ambition to embody these resilience skills - humbly and still with many gaps.

I would like to thank the Favre publishing house for its renewed confidence, in particular Sophie Rossier and Aline Lehmann. Your kindness and your pertinent suggestions throughout the writing process were a precious encouragement. Thanks to Sophie Conchon for her talent as an illustrator and her contagious enthusiasm.

Special thanks to Ilham Kadri and Thomas Buberl, resilient leaders we would like to see more of, for writing the foreword and afterword to this book. Thank you also to the leaders, men, and women, I have been fortunate enough to meet at the various stages of my career. I continue to learn every day by observing those who lead teams, and by trying to learn from their experiences.

My deepest gratitude goes to Dr. Sven Hansen, founder of the Resilience Institute, who foresaw more than twenty years ago how resilience would become a critical skillset to cultivate in the professional world. A huge thank you to all of my colleagues and associates at the Resilience Institute; your commitment, courage and integrity are examples that inspire me every day.

A heartfelt thank you to my parents, Baudouin and Françoise Michiels, and to my four sisters, who support me in all my projects with their unconditional affection. I cannot conclude the list of thanks without mentioning the man I have been in love with for more than thirty years, Benoit Greindl.

His vision of a better future colors every page of this book. My dearest wish is that our four children may live and thrive in a more sustainable, just, and inclusive world.

BIBLIOGRAPHY

- Antonio R. Damasio, *Looking for Spinoza*, Houghton Mifflin Harcourt, 2003
- Bill George, *Authentic Leadership*, Jossey-Bass, 2004
- Boris Cyrulnik, Philippe Bouhours, *Sport et résilience*, Odile Jacob, 2019
- Boris Cyrulnik, *Des saisons et des âmes*, Odile Jacob, 2021
- Brad Hook, *Resilience Mastery: 11 keys to upgrade human performance*, The Resilience Institute, 2019
- Brené Brown, *The power of vulnerability*, Sounds True, 2012
- Brené Brown, *Dare to lead*, Penguin Random House, 2018
- Carol Dweck, *Mindset*, Little Brown Book Club, 2017
- Christophe Haag, *La contagion émotionnelle*, Albin Michel, 2019
- Daniel Goleman, *Emotional intelligence: EQ 2.0*, TH Press, 2019
- Daniel Goleman, Richard Boyatzis, Anne Mc Kee, *Primal Leadership*, Harvard Business Review Press, 2013
- Delphine Batho, *Écologie intégrale*, éd. du Rocher, 2019
- Drs Raphael Heinzer, Jose Haba-Rubio, *Je rêve de dormir*, Favre, 2016
- Edgar Morin, La méthode IV. *Les idées : leur habitat, leur vie, leurs mœurs, leur organisation*, Seuil, 1991
- Gretchen Reynolds, *The First 20 Minutes*, Avery, 2013
- Hector Garcia, Frances Miralles, *Ikigai*, Penguin Life, 2017
- Howard Gardner, *Multiple Intelligences*, Basic Books, 2006
- Joël de Rosnay, *Je cherche à comprendre : les codes cachés de la nature*, Les liens qui libèrent, 2016
- Joël de Rosnay, *La symphonie du vivant : comment l'épigénétique va changer votre vie*, Les liens qui libèrent, 2018
- Johann Hari, *Lost connections*, Bloomsbury, 2018
- Martin Seligman, *Learned optimism*, Vintage, 2006
- Martin Seligman, *Flourish*, Atria, 2012

- Matthieu Ricard, Alexandre Jollien, Christophe André, *Trois amis en quête de sagesse*, L'iconoclaste/Allary, 2016
- Matthieu Ricard, *Altruism*, Back Bay Books, 2016
- Matthew Walker, *Why we sleep*, Scribner, 2018
- Mihaly Csikszentmihalyi, *Flow: the psychology of optimal experience*, HarperCollins, 1991
- Mihaly Csikszentmihalyi, *Good Business: leadership, flow and the making of meaning*, Penguin Books, 2004
- Nicole Huybens, *La forêt boréale, l'éco-conseil et la pensée complexe*, Éditions universitaires européennes, 2010
- Olivier Bourquin, *La performance sur mesure*, Favre, 2014
- Richard J. Davidson, Sharon Begley, *The emotional life of your brain*, Avery, 2012
- Philippe Descola, *Par-delà nature et culture*, Gallimard, 2005
- Viktor E. Frankl, *Man's search for meaning*, Beacon Press, 1959
- Simon Sinek, *Start with why*, Portfolio, 2011
- Stuart Taylor, *Assertive Humility: emerging from the ego trap*, Monterey Press, 2013
- Sven Hansen, *Inside Out: the practice of resilience*, The Resilience Institute, 2015
- Tania Singer, Matthieu Ricard, Kate Karius, *Caring economics*, Picador, 2015
- Yves Citton, *The ecology of attention*, Polity, 2017

Website – sources of inspiration

Betterbusinessact.org

Bcorporation.net

Businessroundtable.org

Circular-economy-switzerland.ch

Climateactiontracker.org

Ec.europa.eu/info/strategy/priorities-2019-2024/europe-an-green-deal_fr

Ellenmacarthurfoundation.org

Ipcc.ch

Paulekman.com

Regenerative-Alliance.org

Resilience-institute-europe.com

Solarimpulse.com

Unfccc.int/climate-action/race-to-zero-campaign

Unfoundation.org

TABLE OF CONTENTS

CHAPTER 4

RELATION WITH THE ENVIRONMENT

CHAPTER 5

THE QUESTION OF MEANING

By the same author

Alexia Michiels

Prefaces by Dr Joel de Rosnay and Dr Sven Hansen

THE RESILIENCE DRIVE

100 simple practices to navigate daily challenges
with joy and success

"A useful and generous book inviting us to experience daily life with joy and awareness"

Frédéric Lenoir

GUIDE
FAVRE